To Gil

JEWS AND GYPSIES

Myths & Reality

Best wishes

Ruth Barnett

1/11/14

Ruth Barnett

This book is dedicated to all the millions of Romanies and Jews, disabled and politically persecuted by the Nazis as 'lives not worthy of life' and to all those whose lives are made miserable by ignorant and prejudiced people today. It is also dedicated to all children and adults willing to think and learn to develop informed opinions so that they can make their lives worthy of living by standing up for those suffering from persecution and racist hatred.

ACKNOWLEDGEMENTS

I would like to thank all those who inspired me not to give up my idea of producing this little book for schools to raise general awareness of the injustice suffered in the past and still being suffered today by Roma and Traveller Gypsies: my family and particularly my son, Bruce Barnett, who did the proof reading; my friends who came round from thinking me crazy to appreciating what I wanted to do; Marina Smith at the Holocaust Centre, Shauna Leven and Simone Abel of Rene Cassin who gave me positive encouragement; and all the teachers I met in the my talks in schools who convinced me this book was needed.

CONTENTS

FOREWORD

Tikkun Olam refers to the obligation of every Jew to work towards repairing the world, to shine light where there is darkness. Few people embody this message of hope like Ruth Barnett. A Holocaust survivor who arrived in the United Kingdom at age four on the Kindertransport, she has dedicated much of her life to ensuring that the atrocities of the Holocaust never happen again. For over two decades, she has told her story to students, journalists, and civic leaders in a quest to stand up for the victims of unjust persecution.

This book embodies her lifelong struggle against the forces of ignorance and fear as they continue to rear their ugly heads in the form of racism and prejudice all over the world. By paralleling the experiences of the Jewish people with those of the Romani people (as Ruth mentions in the text, "Romani" is only one way to refer to this rich and diverse group and I use it here to simplify the text; I otherwise ascribe to the principle which Ruth espouses, to refer to one as they choose to be called), she shows how closely the stories of Europe's most widely persecuted minorities resemble each other.

Perpetrators of large scale atrocities like the Holocaust are often labelled as monsters, seemingly having nothing in common with the rest of us. However their crimes are only ever made possible when good people choose to remain silent. It takes special courage to stand up for those who society maligns the most and Ruth encourages each person to find the inner courage to do so.

Challenging conventional perceptions of Romani people throughout the book, Ruth opens a window to the richness of their culture that is seldom seen by those who do not choose to look. Numerous stories are told about how hope and resilience allowed people to overcome insurmountable challenges and to eventually persevere. These individuals not only became valuable members of their own communities, many have made important contributions to the wider society in they lived. It is important to counter the negative perceptions with positive stories and examples; ultimately the stereotypes will no longer hold. Ruth's training as a teacher and psychotherapist also shines through in the book, in which she engages the reader in a dialogue rather than in a confrontational or dogmatic debate. She accepts that human behaviour does not always make sense, and calmly addresses the subject matter in "plain English" without making tenuous arguments or excuses for failings on either side.

I know Ruth in her capacity as a Romani Rights campaigner for René Cassin, the Jewish human rights organisation. Many Jewish people struggle to explain the inner pressure, almost a compulsion they feel to make the world a better place. This is often explained by referencing history ("I suffered therefore I should work to prevent suffering") or teachings (there are numerous such interpretations of Jewish texts and commentary). I would argue that these factors combined create a set of "Jewish values" that drive some Jewish people like Ruth to work tirelessly on behalf of others. I do not know if Ruth attempts to explain it, but it does not matter; her actions speak for themselves.

Shauna Leven
Executive Director of René Cassin

PREFACE

"Gippoes", "pikeys", "dids" and "scum": "Gypsies, tramps and thieves". Romani people are used to being talked about; used to being constantly referred to in every arena from pub conversations to the national press. Romani people are used to being called by a ragtag assortment of names that may or may not be properly spelled, may or may not have a capital letter, or may be plain old racist slurs. What Romani people are not used to is being talked about in a knowledgeable way: in a way that shows even the slightest awareness of a thousand-and-more year history of a people who never quite seem to fit in, and who have often paid the ultimate price for being different.

I remember the few times Romanies were mentioned at school: in fact, only two occasions stick in my head. The first was at primary school, when the teacher read a poem about a Gypsy stealing a hare, and lying about how it had jumped into his bucket. Later, when we were studying Nazi Germany, I remember reading a long list of groups persecuted by the Nazis. The Jews were at the top, followed by Poles, Black people, communists, those with disabilities, homosexuals, and Jehovah's Witnesses. Then, at the bottom of the list, came the familiar word for my people: the "gypsies". On the one hand, I remember feeling grateful that our people were mentioned at all. I'd seen other books where no mention was made. The message of this list, though, was clear: whether intentional or not, it implied some kind of hierarchy of the victims. The "gypsies" came last, so they can't have suffered that much, and their name didn't start with a capital letter like the Jews and Poles, so they can't have been a 'proper' people, anyway.

Without meaning to, I absorbed this list and what it implied. I did not yet know that the Nuremberg Race Laws stated Jews and "Zigeuner"- the word the Nazis used for Romani people, which originally meant "Untouchables"- to be an equal threat to German racial "purity". I did not know that in Germany, and other countries such as Yugoslavia and Croatia, over three quarters of the Romani population was murdered; or that Romani people had been rounded up, shot and gassed in every corner of Europe from Russia to the French Pyrenees. If Hitler had crossed the Channel, I probably wouldn't be alive to write this. If only there had been a book like Ruth Barnett's when I was at school, not only would we have learnt more fully the awful truth about what happened to Jews and Romanies during the Holocaust. We would have seen how eerily similar some modern people's attitudes towards Romani people, and other ethnic nomads like Irish Travellers, are to those held by the Nazis, and how letting such attitudes flourish is the first step on the awful road to genocide. We would have also seen the positive side: the unheard stories that prove the Nazis were wrong; that stereotypes never give us the bigger picture. We would have heard about Romani orchestras, politics, language and literature; about how Jewish and Romani people have not just shared a history of persecution, but have at times shared their culture through music like Klezmer and Jazz, and sometimes through marriage, as testimonies in this book show.

Many Romanies admire the Jews, seeing in them not only an analogue to their own entrepreneurial culture and survival against the odds, but a people who have shared their deepest sufferings, from the slavery and pogroms of the Middle Ages to the extermination attempt of the twentieth century. It is therefore a source of deep sadness that there has been so little co-operation in remembering the terrible grief of the 1930s and 40s. I hope *Jews and Gypsies: Myths and Realities* will be read as widely as possible, and that the truths it carries will remedy some of these hurts.

Damian Le Bas
Editor, *Travellers' Times*

INTRODUCTION

WHY JEWS AND GYPSIES?

A LOT OF people believe very strange things about Gypsies and Jews and some of these things are what this book aims to explore. People also believe strange, and often negative, things about other groups like Muslims or Asylum-seekers; but this book is about Gypsies and Jews because misunderstanding and persecution of them is so intense and widespread all over Europe and other parts of the world too. The problem is that many people believe things someone tells them or they read in a newspaper without thought or question, especially about Jews and Gypsies. This is usually because they know very little about them. This book will, hopefully, give you, the reader, some understanding of minority groups, like Gypsies and Jews and stimulate you to find out more. A book can only introduce you to a limited amount but there is a huge amount of interesting things about Gypsies and Jews to explore on the Internet. There is a vast number of books written by Jews and a growing number of books written by Gypsies. There are some suggestions for you to begin with in the appendix of this book.

This book is not a scholarly research work with lots of

information, like Ian Hancock's book *We are the Romanies*, which I recommend highly. My intention is to challenge you to think about and question what people tell you about Jews and Gypsies, and that includes reflecting on and questioning what I am telling you in this book. I hope you will want to find out more about Gypsies and Jews from lots of other sources so that you can form your own 'informed' opinion instead of sheepishly believing what one person tells you without checking it out.

Some of you may disagree with things in this book that make you feel uncomfortable, angry or just puzzled. That is good if it challenges you to think, discuss with others and find out more. Some things we can't all agree about and we have to respect each other's opinions. Everyone is entitled to form their own opinion, as long as it is not derogatory, insulting or damaging to other people. Jews and Gypsies don't agree among themselves and there are some groups of each that don't recognise other groups as belonging. But they tend to come together when they are threatened from outside. Gypsies and Jews are the ethnic/cultural minority groups that have been most maligned, hated and persecuted for centuries by Anti-Semitism and Romophobia/ Anti-Gypsyism. In this and many other more positive ways they are similar and that is why I have written this book about both. Of course there are many important differences too.

I am well aware that I risk offending some people who disagree with things I say in this book. It is sometimes not possible to be honest and open without giving offence to some people. I intend to be open and honest in this book because I want to encourage my readers to be open and honest with themselves. I hope anyone who may feel offended will accept that I do not intend to offend or hurt anyone's feelings.

There is a problem with the word 'Gypsy'. It is insulting because it is a label invented by people who were not Roma or Travellers. The Roma, or Romanies as some like to be called, did not choose it themselves. In fact it was ignorant people who thought these people had come from Egypt who called them 'Gypsies' (Egyptians – 'Gyptians' – Gypsies) in the first place. Unfortunately, this label has become the only name for Roma and Travellers that a lot of people understand and they are unaware of just how insulting it is because, on the whole, the Travellers and Roma don't protest and sometimes even use this label themselves in order to communicate and be understood.

What is even more insulting is to write the words 'Gypsy' or 'Gypsies' without a capital letter. A lot of national and local newspapers still don't use capitals for Gypsies and Travellers even though they have been told it is insulting and they would never print Muslim or Jew without a capital. It is rather like calling them animals, sheep or cattle. Without being aware of it, I suspect some of these people actually think of Gypsies as animals. The capital letter recognises them as a Human group and, whatever we may think of them, Roma and Travellers are just as human as you and me and they are part of our community. We need to learn about them and understand their ways so that we can stop isolating them as 'different' and adjust to accepting them as being part of 'us' – part of our "Big Society" and part of the Human Race.

Now that I have explained why the word Gypsy is is insulting, I shall use Roma or Romanies and Travellers most of the time. I hope by the time you come to the end of this book that using the words Traveller, Roma and Romanies will seem natural and the insulting words Gypsy and Gypsies will begin to seem strange and wrong to you. But the problem is more complicated and there is no simple solution. Some people proudly call themselves Gypsies to show that they have risen above insults and prejudice and want to claim control of the name for themselves. They may even feel offended if you don't call them Gypsies. Every person has a right to choose what he or she wants to be called and we should respect his or her decision. I hope you object if someone does not respect how you wish to be called; but I hope you are also careful about what you call other people.

Zigeuner in German, Zigane or Tsiganae in French are even more insulting than Gypsy, because they come from the word 'atsingani' that means 'untouchable'. The most insulting word, used mainly in England against Roma and Travellers, is 'pikey'. It is a strange word that, like 'idiot' and 'imbecile', was once a perfectly good ordinary word until it was used as an insult. It comes from 'turnpike', a word for the toll road or highway. So a pikey would have been someone on the highway. Roma and Travellers have their own word for people who are not Travellers or Roma – Gadje (sometimes spelt in different ways). It simply means 'not a Roma person' and is not insulting in itself, though angry Romanies sometimes use it in an insulting way. I don't like to be called a Gadje or gadje because it is a label from outside and not chosen by me.

It is too easy to hurt people by using words as insults. I sincerely believe that a lot of people have little idea how much they contribute today to the insults and persecution that Roma, Travellers and Jews have suffered for centuries. Many people have told me that this book is necessary to help us to understand what is insulting and hurtful to people who are our fellow human beings. Relatively few folk today care enough about Roma and Travellers to notice how unjustly they are accused of all sorts of things, and how they mostly miss out on education and health services. The more I think and learn about Travellers and Romanies, the more I see similarities with Jews. As a Jew, how can I possibly claim justice for Jews unless I protest at injustice towards other groups?

Of course Jews and Roma are not the only minority groups to have been the target of people's prejudices and persecution. Most people have at least a bit of difficulty with other people who seem to be very different from them. One or two individuals who are very different usually appear interesting; but when there is a large group of people with different skin colour, religion or cultural norms, they can appear threatening and frightening. Gypsies are often seen as a threat to middle class life style and values, and even a threat to their livelihood. This is irrational and unreasonable, just like the Nazi fear of Jews wanting to rule the world. With the world population of 70 billion (in 2010) and the Jewish population of 13.3 million (i.e. 0.19% of the world population), how could Jews possibly take over the world? Prejudice is not reasonable or rational but based on fear, which is an emotion that can become out of control.

This sometimes leads to the whole group being attacked or isolated at the edges of the community. Then everything bad is blamed on them, even when it is absurd to do so. Both Jews and Roma have been ill treated in this way for centuries. Most people know very well that it is illegal as well as immoral or simply wrong to insult or physically attack Jews, Muslims, homosexuals, blind and other disabled people, even if they do so. But a lot of people think it is all right to say nasty things about Gypsies and treat them as if they are inferior. Prejudiced and racist attacks against Roma and Travellers are also illegal but anti-Gypsyism is the last bastion of culturally acceptable racism.

Roma and Travellers are currently the most unjustly persecuted ethnic minority group right across Europe. Many people know very little about Jews, their history and their culture, but it is at least taught in most schools. A lot of people are almost totally ignorant of Roma and Traveller history and culture. This needs to be taught in schools too. Both groups have a fascinating history. When people don't have much real knowledge about something or someone, they tend to believe what someone else says. And if lots of people tell you the same thing about Jews or Travellers and Roma, it starts to feel like "the truth" and you begin to feel that 'they must be like that because everyone says so'. Sadly a lot of things people say, especially about Gypsies and Jews are manufactured truths or myths, or downright lies.

Unscrupulous people use myths as propaganda to control what other people think. So I shall explore myths and realities in this book and I hope this will interest you and encourage you to think about and check out what people tell you (including what I am going to tell you) before you believe it. I have called this book's subtitle "Stereotypes and myths that lead to prejudice and racism" because so often there is no simple single Truth. There are many truths and many realities.

Reality looks quite different depending on from where you are looking at it. Two people describing the same thing or event may have two very different versions, but both are 'true'. I hope you will gain in your understanding of this through reading this book and many other books and, above all, listening to many different people's personal experience rather than settling for believing 'hearsay'.

GYPSIES AND JEWS

Jews and Gypsies are two very different groups of people. But they also have some very interesting similarities, which I shall explore in this book. Both groups originated in the East; the Jews from Mesopotamia and the Holy Land (now Israel-Palestine) and the Roma from what is now North India. We know the history and origin of the Jews from the Bible. Roma did not write books about their history but their origin has been established by tracing the roots of their language, Romanes, to the Sanskrit language of that area of India. The Indian Institute of Romani Studies in London claims that the Indian government should recognise all Roma as non-residents (or expatriates) who left India in the 11th Century. The Roma were originally driven out of India as an 'unwanted' underclass and some may have been brought West as slaves. The original group became split up into many tribes, such as Bantery,

Abdals, Manush, Kalderash, Kali, Sinti, Halabi, Dom, Lom, Roma, Liloro and Romichal. The Sinti tribes lived for centuries mainly in Western Europe and the Roma mainly in Eastern Europe. Sinti comes from Sindh, a province in India where it is believed by some that they originally lived centuries ago.

The Dom, with their own language, Domari, which is related to Romanes or Romani, live mainly in the Middle East. The Jews started in Biblical times with the 12 tribes of Israel. Since the Jews were expelled from the Holy Land, after the destruction of their second temple, they spread westwards. There are now Jewish communities all over the world. These communities make up what is called the Jewish Diaspora. There are groupings that link between the communities, such as the religious affiliations like 'Orthodox' and 'Progressive'.

The Roma communities in all the different countries, not only in Europe, also form a Diaspora. Similar to Jewish communities, there are lots of disagreements, arguments and feuds between their various subgroups; but they unite in the face of persecution and stand up for each other. All Jews define themselves as Jews but some of the subgroups don't consider other subgroups Jews at all. It is rather similar with all these subgroups of Roma. So it is difficult to know what to call them if we mean all of them. In 1971 there was a gathering of Roma in Orpington, UK, and at this Congress they founded the International Romani Union, which has grown into an NGO (non-governmental organisation) that has consultative status at the United Nations and is linked with ERTF – the European Roma and Travellers Forum. They decided to use the name Roma as an umbrella-name to include all the tribes. There is also a Gypsy Council going back to 1966 or even earlier and many other organisations.

Some groups were not represented at the 1971 Congress and don't agree to be called Roma. As Roma is the name the majority chose for themselves, we should respect their choice and use it instead of 'Gypsies'. There are many arguments about whether Travellers come under the umbrella name Roma. Most of the Travellers in Britain originated in Ireland but quite possibly some Roma tribes also reached Ireland. Many groups of Roma have led a travelling life, and some still do. Although the Roma and Travellers are against their people marrying out of their group, there has been a lot of inter-marriage; and even some between Jews and Gypsies. The only real solution is to ask the group you are talking about what they like to be called; but, of course, this is not always possible.

The Roma Union also agreed on a Roma Nation Flag. The blue represents the sky, under which they live; the green represents the green earth over which they travel, and the red sixteen-spoked chakra wheel represents how an important part of their original culture was to live most of the time 'on wheels' in a caravan or chalet.

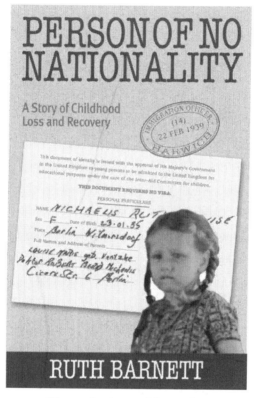

The author's autobiography

CHAPTER 1

HOW DID I COME TO WRITE THIS BOOK?

I WROTE MY first book while I was a secondary school teacher. As a Deputy Head in London I had to take classes that could not be accommodated by other teachers. One of these was the Child Care class for 15 year olds that did not want to do 'academic subjects', and most of them didn't want to do anything at all in school. So I set about engaging their interest. We didn't just learn about babies, I got mothers to come in with real babies and we went out to maternity units and nurseries. We didn't just learn about baby books and baby toys, we made books and went into playgroups to read them to real toddlers; and we brought the toddlers into our school to watch a puppet show of the toys we had made. I changed the class name to Child Development and we studied the life cycle, from childhood through adolescence to adulthood and closing the cycle with child-rearing. I wrote the first ever British school textbook on Child development, "People Making People: child development in context", published in 1985, just before I left teaching in 1986 and became a psychotherapist.

In 1991 Holocaust education was made a requirement in the national curriculum. The teachers at that time had no formal Holocaust education themselves to equip them for this sensitive difficult topic. They needed help. So I joined a group of Holocaust Survivors willing to go into schools and talk with teachers and their students about our own experiences. Teachers and students found this so interesting and inspiring that many of us have continued to go into schools and other gatherings ever since. I found I could never tell my story in enough detail in the hour to 90 minutes I was given and there was never enough time to answer all the students' questions and hear their comments. So I decided to write a second book. As the students always liked my description of living on a farm with all the animals during wartime in Sussex, I included many stories of animals on the farm. The Nazis took German nationality away from all German Jews in 1933. So I had no nationality for the first eighteen years of my life until I could become British in 1953. That is why I called my second book *Person of No Nationality*. It was published in 2010. This book made quite an impact and, although I had written it for schoolchildren, it seemed to resonate with the child inside every adult, too. By this time I was not only telling my own story as a Kindertransportee (Kinder = German for children), but trying to get students to think of the implications in terms of which children today might be suffering because of other peoples' prejudice and persecution. I started asking groups who were the people nobody liked and even hated and were nasty to in their own locality. Time and again they would tell me how the Gypsies were hated because they were 'so dirty and such a nuisance'. I encouraged them to think about what evidence they had for this image. I challenged them to consider whether perhaps Travellers consider non-Travellers a nuisance; and to imagine themselves being treated like the Travellers in their area were being treated and how this might feel, such as being called 'dirty Gypsies' instead of what they call themselves - Roma or Travellers.

One thoughtful youngster, in a group I was talking with, asked me "What do you know about Gypsies, Miss?" I told him all I knew about them in my childhood when they were a very important part of the rural economy. Crops would not have been planted or harvested without Roma and Travellers moving round the country to where the work was needed. They made baskets, clothes pegs, sharpened knives and made all sorts of craft produce. The village blacksmith was a Romani who was very friendly when I took the farm horses to be shod. But I had to admit I had not met any Roma or Travellers for about 50 years. That dialogue made me decide that I needed to learn about modern Travellers and Roma. I got myself an introduction to Dale Farm and I was horrified to learn how badly they were treated. I did what I could to support and encourage them. They fought Basildon Council for ten years in the courts against eviction from the piece of land they had bought as a junkyard and had made habitable at their own expense.

In my talks I told my audiences what I had learnt from visiting Dale Farm, reading email newsletters from the Roma Virtual Network and talking to various people working with Roma and Travellers. I then challenged them to compare this with how the Nazis started treating the Jews - more or less how we are treating Travellers and Roma right now. It was only when the Nazis realised that nobody cared enough about Jews and Gypsies to intervene that they began planning to wipe them out. The more I thought about it the more similarities I found between Gypsies and Jews. That was why I decided to write my third book about Jews and Gypsies. There are some similarities in the culture the two ethnic groups have developed, but also huge differences; and there are striking similarities in the history of these two peoples, which I will explore in this book.

I hope by the time you have read it, you will agree that this book is necessary to get people thinking about their stereotyped images and wanting to understand a bit more about Roma, Travellers and Jews.

CHAPTER 2

WHO AND WHAT IS A JEW? WHO ARE THE ROMANIES?

IDENTITY IS VERY important. We need to know who and what we are so that we can form an identity that we can feel comfortable about owning. Unless I am comfortable with who I am, how can I possibly relate comfortably with others? When you know who you are and are comfortable with being who you are, you might enjoy helping others to find out who they are.

Who you are is at first mostly to do with the family you are born into and where your family came from. As a young child you take for granted who you are. Your parents and siblings treat you in a way that tells you who you are. You don't really think about it until you find you are called names or excluded from something –just because of who you are.

I was a baby, 8 months old, when the Nazis took away German nationality – citizenship – from all the Jews. The Nazis decided who was a Jew and who was not. Because I had a Christian mother and a Jewish father, the Nazis decided I was Jewish and not good enough to be a member of the Aryan 'master-race' that the Nazis wanted to create. They decided to kill all the Jews, Sinti and Roma, as they imagined them to have poisonous blood that would spoil the 'purity' of their 'master-race'. All this was an evil myth that that the Nazis deliberately created and I will discuss it further in a later chapter.

As I described in my previous book *Person of No Nationality*, I had to flee from Germany, otherwise the Nazis would have murdered me. Britain rescued 10,000 children from Nazi persecution by bringing them to England on the Kindertransport. My brother aged seven and I at age four were two of those children. Because I was born in Germany and was kicked out as a non-citizen, I thought there must be something wrong with me. Of course people in England were very anti-German during the war and that made me feel ashamed of having come from Germany. I simply wanted to be English and accepted, like everyone else. That is what young children usually want most of all – to be like everyone else and to be respected and accepted as such. That is what Jewish and Gypsy children want too. I avoided talking about my German roots and disowned them. But you can't do that because you are not a whole person if you disown a part of yourself. Disowning your roots makes you extra vulnerable, like a tree with no roots. The next storm is likely to blow it over. Without your roots you might be emotionally blown over by the ordinary difficulties of life.

I think it is very sad that some children today are made

Person well-rooted in
the family can stand up
to an emotional storm

Person cut off from the family
roots is traumatised by the
emotional storm

to feel ashamed of who they are and where their families have come from. Everyone should be able to own their roots, their family history, and be proud of who they are. If you have relatives in another country you are doubly rich; you have the heritage of the country you are growing up in, but also that of the country your family came from. You should be able to be proud of your entire heritage. Some children hide their roots because ignorant people tease and persecute them about it. Sometimes it is because the persecutors are envious; when you think someone else has something good that you think you can never have for yourself you get urges to attack and destroy it so that nobody can have it.

Jews and Roma are not the only peoples to be hated and persecuted but these two groups both have long histories of being unwanted and driven away by their local communities for no other reason than who they are. The Nazis and their collaborators murdered at least half a million Roma and Sinti as well as about six million Jews. The victims were children, women and men, all human people like you and me. Because they hated the Roma and Jews, the Nazis took the opportunity to get rid of them under the cover of WWII, as there was no-one willing to stop them. A lot of people dislike or even hate Jews today but they know it is wrong to attack and persecute them and that the police will stop them. But a lot of people today think it is OK to hate Roma and Travellers, to say nasty things about them, treat them badly and drive them away. Mostly, the Travellers and Roma don't report attacks. It is usually the police who are called in to evict or drive Travellers away when they have settled on land without permission. So how can they trust the police? But where are they to go when there is nowhere where they can get permission to be?

When there was nowhere for the Jews and Gypsies of Europe to go, because no country wanted to give them refuge, the Nazis decided to round them all up, put them in cattle trucks and deport them to killing camps in Eastern Europe, mainly Poland. Many of those who escaped or survived had great difficulty coming to terms with the horrors they experienced. Today Jewish survivors are accepted as a valuable part of their communities. However, Roma today are being rounded up again, their homes bulldozed away or torched, and driven away or deported, just like in the time of the Nazis. France has been deporting Gypsies since 2010. Campsites have been burnt or smashed in many countries. Some Roma are treated very badly in every European country and many other parts of the world.

In England there have been many evictions of Traveller communities. Usually people don't even notice or don't protest even when they do. The eviction of Dale Farm was such a brutal eviction, with over 100 riot police with stun guns, that it hit the British national news and was shown on

TV in many other countries as well. The early stages of the Holocaust are being repeated in front of our eyes, and not by Nazis, but by us. This includes you and me if we close our eyes to it and don't protest.

What we are is a different matter. By discovering our family tree and learning our family history, we can know who we are. There is a TV programme many people enjoy *Who do You Think You Are?* Some people get real surprises when they research their ancestors and discover all sorts of interesting people in their family tree. Our identity, or what we are, is quite different and mostly up to us to determine. Have you been asked or asked yourself "What do I want to be?" Your teachers at school will at some time in your schooling talk with you about all the possible careers you might think about. But what sort of a person are you, what sort of a person do you want to be? It helps to have already owned all of who you are, and be comfortably proud of it, as a foundation for developing what you are going to be.

I hope this book will help you to think about yourself in relation to other people, specifically in relation to Jews and Roma. If you are Jewish or Romani, I hope you are comfortable with that and proud of your family and background. If you are not a Romani or Jewish person, I hope this book will encourage you to learn about Jews and Roma. I intend it to help you to develop into a person who does not pre-judge people before you even meet them (pre-judging is what prejudice means). I hope it will help you to gather a lot of information from different sources before you make up your own mind about who and what a Romani or Jewish person is. If you can master the tendency to pre-judge, which is in all of us, and master the urge to look down on people less fortunate than yourself, then what you will be is a much nicer and probably happier person, than if you don't care to think and learn but just want to vent your negative thoughts and feelings on any suitable scapegoat. Yes, there are some Jews, Roma and Travellers who are scruffy unsavoury-looking people and some who are thieves and cheats. The majority are not like that. Most of them are ordinary decent people and some of them are talented and highly successful in all sorts of activities, trades ad professions. That goes for just about every group of people, including whatever group you belong to yourself.

CHAPTER 3

MONSTERS

MONSTERS ARE MYTHOLOGICAL creatures that belong in legends and stories. They are huge, freakish, unnatural, scary, sometimes cuddly and sometimes horribly evil, usually powerful and they amaze us. That is why we love stories and films about monsters, such as The Big Friendly Giant, Where the Wild Things Are, Dinosaurs, King Kong and 'Baddies that do terrible things but are eventually conquered by the 'Goodies'. While they are safely in stories, we can indulge our imagination in the world of make-believe and enjoy the monsters.

When we bring monsters into the real world it can become very dangerous, especially when reality and fiction become confused. How often have you heard someone called a monster? Is that person really a monster or has she or he done something freakish or unacceptable, unnatural or even evil? It is the action that is monstrous not the person.

Each and every one of us has a 'monster' inside us that sometimes urges us to do something monstrous. Mostly we don't do these monstrous actions because we have learnt to control our 'monster' – we think before we act. Sometimes a person thinks everyone else has done something exciting and adventurous but bad and dangerous, and so they do it – and afterwards they discover it was all bravado and no-one else actually did it.

Sometimes we are persuaded and even become convinced that a person is a monster or a group of people are monsters. This is usually because somebody tells us distorted or untrue things because they want us to think these people are monsters. This is propaganda and, if we believe it without bothering to think for ourselves, we become prejudiced. Prejudice means pre-judging – judging and making up our minds without thinking and finding out if it's true or even reasonable. We all pre-judge to some extent. But most of us are willing to give 'the benefit of the doubt' to a person someone says is bad until we meet that person and find out for ourselves. But propaganda can be very powerful. If lots of people say the same thing, we find it hard not to believe it. If a Jew or a Roma person has cheated has cheated you or done you a personal injury, it is appropriate to be furious and reasonable to feel angry with the one who injured you. But it is not reasonable to be angry with and hate everyone in that group. Prejudice is to hate more than is reasonable.

Terrible things were said about Jews in many parts of the world for centuries before the Nazis existed. However the Nazis built on the existing anti-Jewish prejudice and myths by creating Jewish monsters in cartoon form in newspapers like Julius Streicher's "Der Stuermer" and on posters telling the non-Jewish Aryan Germans lies about Jews.

NAZI CHARICATURE OF A JEW

Streicher's Jews were all pot-bellied, richly clothed and be-jewelled and very ugly and frightening with huge noses. This was manufacturing 'truths' of such exaggerated proportions that it really was amazing how people at that time believed these monster-Jews actually existed. Perhaps, as there is no easy way of telling who is a Jew, people were frightened of the monster-Jews they thought existed but they had never met. Of course, the propaganda was to make people think that all Jews were monsters. This was to make them want to get rid of the Jews and help the Nazis to do just this. As the hatred, fuelled by propaganda, increased, people either didn't mind or actually supported the Nazis ill-treating, persecuting and finally killing Jews.

In the past there were myths about rather romantic Monster Gypsies who seduced wealthy ladies with their Gypsy-music and carried them off. The Nazis considered Zigeuner (Sinti and Roma) to be a 'social nuisance' that would spoil the pure blood of the Aryan Master-race. They convinced the population that they must be rid of the Sinti and Roma as well as the Jews. That is how what the Roma call Porrajmos and the rest of us call the Holocaust happened – when too many people believed the distortions and lies and had neither the courage to care nor the will to act against it.

THE
ROMANTIC
SEDUCTIVE
FANTASY
OF
THE
GYPSY
MUSICIAN

Authors writing articles or books about the Holocaust sometimes call the Nazis monsters. Cartoons often depict Nazis as larger than life and with ugly scowls and threatening postures. Some people like to think of the Nazis as monsters because that makes them different and unlike us, who are not monsters.

But the Nazis were not monsters; they were real people, not cartoon caricatures. Some of them did some very monstrous evil things. But all the Nazis and their helpers and followers were ordinary human beings like you and me. All of us, including you and me, have the capacity to become a murderous Nazi. But we also have the capacity to become a thoughtful, kind and compassionate person. Most of us want to be the latter and so we reflect on our bad or evil urges and control them. Most people find power attractive and are fascinated by people who have or had great power even if they abused their power to do evil things. It is part of our human make-up to be interested and excited by violence and evil. We are not responsible for our interests, thoughts and feelings. They just come in us. But we ARE responsible for how we act on these.

The Nazis' invented Jewish 'monsters' that were very powerful and were trying to rule the world, which is really what the Nazis wanted to do themselves.

NAZI MONSTER

An ordinary looking Nazi

The Nazis were powerful enough to dominate most of Europe to the extent that few people dared to stand up to them. By comparison Sinti and Roma presented no imagined threat at all. Quite the opposite; Nazi myths about Roma showed them as weak and slovenly characters that were dirty and disgusting and deliberately encouraged other people to look down on them as inferior. Sadly, a lot of people still regard Roma just as the Nazis did. We have not yet learned the lessons of the Holocaust and Porrajmos.

The truth about monsters is that they don't exist in reality. They only exist in people's minds. We are all just human beings, even though some behave so badly towards others that their victims experience them as frightening monsters. Somebody else's hatred towards you can feel terrifying, especially when you know that you have done nothing to deserve their hatred. If they hate you just because of who you are (just because you are Jewish or a Romani), not anything you have done, that is bewilderingly fearful. Fearful, because you can't say sorry and make amends when you haven't deserved their hateful rage; and bewildering because it is not rational. Prejudice and racist hatred are irrational and unreasonable.

CHAPTER 4

MYTHS

BOTH JEWS AND Gypsies are experienced as different to the majority of the European population. When we meet one person who looks different, that usually strikes us as interesting and perhaps makes us want to investigate and even make friends with her or him. But if we meet a whole group of people that seem different, or such a group suddenly comes to live in our area, we are more likely to experience them as a threat, as frightening or suspicious. Instead of wanting to make friends, we want to drive them away by teasing, laughing at or harassing them to make them go away. Such behaviour can make a frightened person feel big and brave and superior to the group they find frightening. But it tends to generate suspicion and anger in the persecuted group and, because we don't know much about them, we imagine things about them and create myths about them, usually very negative ones. Too many people are all too ready to believe what someone else says about others, or what the newspapers say, rather than checking whether it is true or even whether it makes sense. There are lots of such myths about Jews, Travellers and Roma.

MYTHS ABOUT RELIGION

Some people believe that the Jewish religion, Judaism, is ancient and out-dated and so it can't be true any longer because Christianity has taken over and is the modern religion and so it must be better. Both Christianity and Judaism go back a long way, and both have many different versions, some of which are more modern and some more 'traditional'. There are some very weird myths, going back to the Middle Ages, about Jews killing children to use their blood for religious purposes. This 'blood libel' originated in 1144 when a young boy, William of Norwich, was found murdered and local Jews were blamed. Though proved to be untrue, people were scared and it led to other murders being blamed on Jews; consequently Jews were persecuted, ostracised and murdered.

Another myth is that Jews killed God and therefore all Jews are guilty of deicide. The Christian story is that the Roman Governor of Judea, Pontius Pilate, gave the Jews the choice between killing Jesus and killing Barrabus, a convict. This is a story that makes no sense. A Roman Governor would give no such choice; Barrabus and Jesus were both Jews as well as the crowd that was supposed to have chosen who was to die. The Christian religion is based on the need for Jesus to die to atone for all the sins of the world. The deicide makes sense as a retrospective story: the Roman Emperor Augustus would not have embraced Christianity if a Roman Governor had murdered the central figure, Jesus. So 'the Jews' had to be blamed instead.

The most pernicious myth about Gypsies is that they have no religion, that they are 'heathen' or 'pagan' barbaric infidels. In fact most Gypsies take religion very seriously. Most but not all Travellers and Roma are Catholic or Eastern Orthodox Christians, but some are Muslim or other religions. Travellers usually have their religious icons in their caravans and attend local churches. Because they take religion seriously, they generally have a high standard of morals and values centred on the family. Just like the myth of Jews stealing children to use their blood for religious rituals, there is also a myth that Roma steal children or put spells and curses on them.

MYTHS ABOUT IDENTITY

Many people think they can tell a Jew or a Romani by looking at them. If you imagine a Jewish or Romani person in your mind, unless you think of one you have come to know well, it is likely to be a stereotype. You might then discover that few actual Jews and Roma fit your stereotypes. We all build up images in our minds from what we have heard from other people plus a bit of our own imagining that we add. Unless we test out these images in reality, they remain stereotypes. And there are some very ugly negative stereotypes that unthinking people actually believe – such as that Gypsies have little or no brains and therefore cannot be educated. Negative stereotypes about Jews include that they have horns have horns like the devil and have a smell that distinguishes them as Jews.

Some Roma and Jews wear very distinctive clothes that are quite different to what most people wear. But a lot of Jews and Roma wear ordinary clothes similar to other people in their locality. Many young people wear distinctive clothes to stand out and look different or to show they belong to a particular group. Some Roma and Travellers live in caravans and travel around wheeler dealing. But so do many people who are not Roma or Travellers. You may have enjoyed travelling round in a caravan yourself on holiday. So people in a caravan are not necessarily Roma or Travellers.

So how can you really tell if someone is Jewish or Romani? The Nazis considered that both Jews and Roma were inferior 'races' with inferior blood that would spoil or poison the 'pure' German Aryan blood. So they decided to get rid of all the Jews (Juden) and Roma (Zigeuner) in Germany and they planned to make the whole of Europe free of Jews and Roma. To do this, the Nazis tried to find a way of identifying who was Jewish or Romani by measuring their heads and noses, but it didn't really work. So they made people prove their blood was 'pure' by producing birth certificates and family trees to show that they had no Jewish or Romani ancestors. Those who couldn't prove this were in great danger if they stayed in Germany and the countries the Nazis occupied, and so many emigrated. It was much more difficult for Sinti and Roma to leave than for Jews.

The Nazis did not invent the theory of inferior and superior 'races'. It goes much further back. In the nineteenth century, Britain, France, Holland, Belgium and Portugal were busy building empires of colonies abroad, particularly in Africa. Because the African peoples had different languages and cultures, white colonisers could not understand them or their culture and regarded them as inferior and barbaric. In fact many of the African peoples had very complex cultures with high standards of morality and pride in their way of life. But the colonisers considered themselves superior and this led to the idea of 'white supremacy' and the slave trade.

In North America the theme of 'white supremacy' led to the slaughter of the native 'Red Indians'(another name which those labelled as such did not choose for themselves) and the Ku Klux Klan that terrorised black African-Americans. In Australia the white settlers slaughtered the native Aborigines who they considered inferior. Actually these original Australian people were very friendly and gentle. They called themselves 'the Dream People'. All in all, the behaviour of white ethnic groups has not been superior at all but exploitative, unjust and murderous. Germany too, had colonies in South West Africa and behaved arrogantly deceitfully and murderously towards the native peoples. The first genocide of the twentieth century was perpetrated by German colonists against the Nama and Hereroes of what is today Namibia. Many people don't know about the bad things that white peoples did in the past and don't want to hear anything bad about the group they belong to. But that does not undo the terrible things that were done There is hardly a country in the world that does not have bits of its history that are unjust and shameful.

Forgetting about or denying that the bad things ever happened is not the answer. The past cannot be wiped out and history cannot be re-written, although that is just what some people try to do. The only way is to bear knowing and learning about the past so that, hopefully, we can do better for the future. If we don't know where we have come from, we can't know where we are now and we have little chance of creating a better future.

A famous philosopher, Santayana, said that those who can't remember the past are doomed to repeat it. We have been repeating myths, prejudices, racism and slaughter and are still doing so today. But, amazingly, the Human Race is still there.

So there must have been a lot of sensitive compassionate people doing their best to comfort the oppressed and heal the traumatised survivors of human atrocities. I try to be one of the healers not one of the persecutors. I hope this book may encourage you to join me in protesting whenever people are being treated violently and unfairly by other people who are prejudiced against them.

Just as the idea of a superior 'master-race' is myth, so is the idea of a 'pure race'. In fact there is only one Human Race. All the other so-called 'races' are ethnic/cultural groups not races. You can leave the ethnic/cultural group you were born into and join another one. Many people do this through inter-marriage. But you can't leave the Human Race and join another race; we are all members of the one Human Race all our lives. Ethnic/cultural groups intermarry and produce what we call 'mixed race' children; so no group remains 'pure' for long.

Orthodox Jews don't accept Liberal and Progressive Jews as 'real' Jews and there is a somewhat similar divisiveness between Roma, Sinti, Travellers and other groupings within these groups. So-called 'authorities' try to decide who is and who isn't Jewish or Romani, but mostly people define themselves by developing their own personal identity, especially if they are proud of their roots and heritage. Part of accepting other people as equal human beings is to accept how they identify themselves instead of trying to impose an identity on them.

MYTHS ABOUT LIFESTYLE

Hitler and his Nazi Party were contemptuous of Jews and Roma because they possessed no land. Only peoples that had a national homeland were worthy of life. They decided that Roma and Jews only deserved to live as long as they could be useful to the Third Reich as slave workers. Because they were 'wandering nomadic peoples', Roma and Jews were considered by the Nazis to be parasites on other peoples lands, draining the life-blood out of other peoples. The reality was that Roma and Jews contributed a lot to the German economy and culture and had fought valiantly for Germany in WWI. The Nazis were not interested in Judaism or the Sinti and Roma Christian religion. The Nazis had their own ideology that was virtually a religion based on purity of blood (the Aryan Master-race), possession of land (Lebensraum) and worship of legendary heroes who had died for Germany.

Many Roma and Jews, probably the majority, have adopted the life style of the country and locality where they live. But some have formed tightly-knit closed communities either to preserve their religion (religiously Orthodox Jews), to preserve their itinerant way of life (Roma and Travellers) or for protection against intense hostility and persecution (Roma and Travellers).

Tight-knit exclusive communities feel threatening to the local people who are excluded because they do not realise that they have excluded the Roma and Travellers. Many people ridicule and attack religious Jews because they feel excluded and frightened of them. Local people often gang up against Travellers and Roma and drive them away. Then they claim that Roma and Travellers are anti-social and only keep to themselves! How can they do otherwise if they are hated and persecuted and can't even trust the police to protect them? It is the job of the police to protect everybody and they take this seriously. But the police also have to evict Travellers form illegal sites. How can Travellers trust the police who evict them? And it is a very dubious job that the police have to do in evicting them when they know there is nowhere for them to go.

There are undoubtedly some Traveller and Roma cheats and thieves. There is a myth that thieving and cheating is in their genes so that they can't do anything else. This is a very stupid and hurtful myth. The reality is that there are far more cheats and thieves who are not Roma or Travellers, some of whom are very talented hard-working people. But when something is stolen or things go wrong, someone blames the 'Gypsies' and others believe it and spread the myth.

When a group of Travellers visit a place, people say the crime rate goes up and blame the Travellers. It may be true that the crime rate goes up and some Travellers may be part of this. But usually there just aren't enough Travellers to commit all the crimes they are accused of. One possible reason for this is that the local criminals take the opportunity to extend their activities when they know the Travellers will be blamed. We all need to be very careful about imposing such a negative identity on any group just because of hearsay about crimes and cheating. There seems to be a high proportion of Roma and Travellers in the figures for petty crime arrests; but there is also a low proportion of them in the figures for more serious crimes.

Some Romanies have included what we call petty thieving in their culture but, for them, this is not thieving but 'living by their wits'. A nomadic life-style used to mean living off the land – land that was there for everybody to use. But now, all the 'common land' has been enclosed and is owned by someone.

Living on fruits, nuts, roots and wild animals is hardly possible anywhere. So when they are refused enough legal places for their caravans and refused employment, where are they to go and how are they to live? Identifying them as 'illegal', 'thieves' and 'a nuisance' is not going to resolve the problem we have with the Roma and Traveller members of our communities. Treating them with respect as equal human beings and consulting with them about the problems is more likely achieve progress.

Hitler blamed two world wars on the Jews and claimed that Jews caused everything that went wrong for Germany in his propaganda speeches. Any thinking person could work out that such a tiny proportion of the population, as the Jews were, could not possibly have the power to do all that damage. But many beliefs are irrational and don't make sense. Even now some people believe that all Jews are cheats because they are all 'stinking rich' and must have cheated somehow to gather such wealth. A little thought reveals that not all Jews are rich; most are just ordinary or average and some are very poor. But people tend to be envious of those who seem to have so much more than themselves. Envy is corrosive; it eats into you and makes you want to attack and destroy those you envy. Some people, who want to justify their hatred towards Jews, have created a myth that Jews are making an 'industry' out of the Holocaust to make money for themselves. Some even claim that the Holocaust never happened and was invented by Jews. It is amazing what myths people create and other people believe without thinking or checking.

There are myths about how Roma are born stupid and devious and are only able to thieve and cheat, whereas Jews are imagined to be born highly intelligent but greedy for greedy for money and become rich through big business and cheating. A few individuals fit these stereotypes and so keep the stereotypes going. Most Roma and Jews don't fit these stereotypes. Once they access enough education, many Roma and Travellers use their intelligence and potential to develop careers and contribute to the community. Roma were skilled craftsmen and women for centuries but not educated. Their native crafts have been largely mechanised and industrialised. Most employers won't hire them and they lose out on education through intense prejudice and persecution. Jews, in comparison developed their intellect as 'the people of the Book' rather than manual skills. So they are perceived as highly intelligent and envied for this. Although people may be largely unaware of their envy, it fuels prejudice and hostility. Both Roma and Jews are envied. Jews are envied for what is seen as their unfair intelligence and nepotism.

Roma are envied for their imagined freedom: freedom to roam under the sun and sleep under the stars, freedom from the law and all the pressures and frustrations of ordinary living. All this is mostly fantasy, fantasies of what we would like to have or be. And then, because we can't have our fantasised wishes, we become envious because we believe the Jews and/or the Roma really have it all. Envy brings up unpleasant, even unbearable, feelings in us, which we then get rid of by projecting them into a scapegoat such as Jews and

Roma. We then perceive Jews or Roma in terms of all the negative traits that we do not want to own in ourselves. There is a nice contradiction here: we perceive Jews and Roma unfairly being and having all the good things we envy while at the same time they are everything bad we can think of! That is how myths grow and thrive.

MYTHS ABOUT POWER AND INFLUENCE

Intense envy and hatred of Roma and Jews has led to two very powerful myths that seem to be so ingrained in our collective psyche or culture that many otherwise sensible and thoughtful people subscribe to them and keep them going.

The first is about a book *The Protocols of the Learned Elders of Zion*.

It was first published in Russia in 1903 and claimed to be the minutes of a meeting of 300 powerful Jewish men setting out plans for taking over and ruling the World. This book was investigated several times (particularly by The Times in 1921) and each time found to be a fraud based on an 1864 French political satire by Maurice Joly *Dialogue in Hell between Machiavelli and Montesquieu* and a German anti-Semitic tract of 1872, "Biarritz" by Hermann Goedsche. Because attraction to conspiracy theories is a human weakness people still believe the myth about Jews seeking to rule the world. The world population reached seven billion in 2010 while the Jewish population worldwide was about 13 million. So how could less than 2% rule the whole 7 billion? Myths are not based on rational thinking but on irrational prejudice. Secondly, a major myth about Roma and Travellers is that they are dirty, 'spoil the countryside' and cause disease to spread. There are certainly some slovenly people in the community that don't keep to the standards expected. But they are certainly not all Roma and Travellers who are usually extremely clean and very house-proud. The big chalet caravans are beautiful inside with modern furniture and attractive ornaments and fittings and they are kept immaculately clean. The reality is that Roma and Travellers have rules and rituals about hygiene and cleanliness that are of a higher standard than the average population. Nevertheless ignorant prejudiced people still believe Travellers and Roma are dirty, unhygienic and uncivilised. People object that Travellers' caravan sites are an 'eyesore' but you seldom hear holiday caravan sites along the coast called an 'eyesore' even if they spoil the coastal views.

Perhaps the most bigoted myth of all is that Roma contribute nothing to the community; that they take up benefits and steal whenever they can without giving anything to the community. As one Romani person told me, "If we are poor they say it's because we don't want to work; and if we are rich they say it's because we steal!" Only ignorant unthinking people believe all Gypsies are like this. The real problem is that many of the Roma who have given a lot to the community are not known as Roma. This is partly because many Romanies prefer their identity to be unknown to avoid harassment by prejudiced people. It is also because the press largely ignores Roma unless they can report negative stories about them. To redress the balance, the Roma Virtual Network (romale@zahav.net.il) sends out emails reporting positive stories of Roma as well as the current injustices against them. There are also many websites created recently by Roma and Travellers. For example www.cingeneyiz.org is one that gives a positive report was about the Sulubba Gypsies called the "Gypsy Doctors of the Desert". Their healing mission is a fine contribution to humanity. Another, by the Roma Daily News email in June 2011, described Pope Benedict XVI meeting 1,500 Romani pilgrims on the 150th anniversary of the birth of Ceferino Gimenez Malla, the first Roma saint. Pope John Paul II beatified him on May 4th 1997. His Romani name is El Pele, the brave one. You can find his whole story on the Internet. The reality is that some Roma have entered into most walks of life, particularly the worlds of music and entertainment. Piroscha Triska, a German-born member of the musical Triska dynasty, was awarded the 2012 Romane Romnija prize. Django Reinhardt is famous in the jazz world. Johann Trollman was an unbeatable boxer in the 1930s, winning over the Nazi's best challengers. This, sadly, meant his death at the hands of the Nazis. Tyson Fury is a current Traveller and a successful boxer. There is a Sinti and Roma Philharmonic orchestra in Frankfurt, Germany, that has composed a new Requiem for Auschwitz that was premiered in Amsterdam in May 2012. The generosity of the Roma in giving to the community is exemplified by the dedication of this Requiem, not to their own Sinti and Roma victims, but to ALL victims of Auschwitz.

It is impossible not to see how much has been given to the community by Jews as this is so well documented in the media and books. Nevertheless, prejudiced people can be heard to say, "Jews make money out of us and give it only to their own people", which of course is nonsense and simply shows ignorance. There are already plenty of books about the Jewish contribution to humanity. We need many more books written by Roma, about the Travellers and Romanies who have greatly benefited the community.

CHAPTER 5

THE LAW-BREAKER MYTH AND THE STORY OF DALE FARM

"The law is an ass," Mr. Bumble in Charles Dickens' Oliver Twist

"… a new covenant; not of the letter, but of the spirit: for the letter killeth, but the spirit giveth life," 2 Corinthians 3:6 English Revised Version

ONE OF THE stereotypes many people have in their minds is that 'all Gypsies are thieves'. Some Roma and Travellers certainly are thieves – but it is patently absurd to extend this to all of them. And, of course, there are many more thieves who are not Romanies. Unfortunately, local people tend to blame any theft and robberies on the Roma or travellers by convincing each other "it's those Gypsies again!" and sometimes that means that thieves who are not Gypsies get away with it. Most Romany families are decent people and have high moral standards, particularly about cleanliness and stealing. Romany mothers would be absolutely furious and make their children take anything stolen back, so that they learn from very young.

In the past, there was plenty of 'common land' and places where nobody minded who caught rabbits and took firewood. 'Helping themselves' as the Roma and Travellers saw it, was for many of them the only way they could survive. Where local populations are very hostile to Roma and Travellers, there are very few opportunities for them to make a living, even just to feed their families. Breaking the law then becomes the only way to survive when the law is heavily weighted against them.

Very few people, who are not trained in law, understand the complications of the legal system and how laws are made and applied. There is no magic that creates perfect laws. People make laws and people sometimes make mistakes. Drafts are written by committees and then submitted to parliament and, after 'due process' they become part of 'the law of the land. The people who are involved in making the laws may have ideas and interests that are very different to those of some of the people affected by the laws. There is a proverb that 'all are equal in the eyes of the law'. This is true in theory; but the reality is different. Wealthy people can and do buy privileges that poorer people simply can't pay for.

Unfortunately, too many clever lawyers are more interested in making big money than in finding the truth and bringing about justice. This means that those who can afford to employ expensive lawyers are more likely to get what they claim, than those who do not have much money. This is not always fair or 'real justice'. There is not nearly enough Legal Aid available, and poor people can usually only get lawyers who cannot compete with the expensive ones. Parliament passes some laws that are unfair and even stupid. Tax laws are very complicated and many people make a career out of interpreting them. Some are honest accountants who help people understand the complexities. Some are not so honest, and work out ways to avoid paying their fair share of taxes. This is legal – the law allows it – but is it fair? Is it moral? You may well ask why don't the law-makers make the tax laws moral as well legal? Politics becomes involved. Those who benefit by an unfair or immoral law don't want it changed and will do all they can to block it.

Prejudices deeply ingrained in the community inevitably affect both the making of laws and how they are interpreted and used. There is a widely believed myth that all Gypsies are law-breakers because it is in their genes and in their culture to flout the law and get away with it. This implies that they are somewhat uncivilised, unsocialised and even unsocialisable. The truth is that it is part of human nature that we are all tempted to take or do things we know we shouldn't.

We sometimes give in to that temptation but we don't like to think of ourselves as 'law-breakers', so we make ourselves feel better by projecting it onto the Roma and

Travellers, so that they are the law-breakers and we are good law-abiding citizens! Also some people envy how they imagine Travellers and Jews are able to 'get away with it' and that makes them want to punish and hurt them with insults.

Because they are denied many of the opportunities and status that the law gives everyone else, some Roma and Travellers become angry and resentful. People, who don't understand what makes them feel this way, experience Travellers and Roma as uncooperative, unsociable and even a 'social nuisance'. Nobody wants a 'social nuisance' and so they clammer for them 'to be removed'. Those who want Travellers removed, don't see them as ordinary people like themselves. They conveniently forget that the law and Human Rights don't just apply to those you like and not to those you don't like. Human Rights have to apply to everybody; you can't divide people into those who deserve Human Rights and those who don't. If you don't stand up for the rights of all people, even ones you don't much care for, then how can you expect people to stand up for you? (Pastor Niemoeller wrote a famous poem about this – see in the Appendix)

PLANNING LAW

In October 2011, just before the brutal eviction of the Dale Farm Travellers, the Prime Minister, David Cameron, made an announcement in parliament with the TV cameras on him that the Travellers must obey the law like everyone else. Of course, this statement is correct. But it is also an unfair political ploy. Everyone should obey the law as long as it is justly applied. Planning Law is very complicated. Few people know enough of the details to understand that local councils who regard Travellers as a 'problem' they want to be rid of, interpret Planning Law against Travellers' interests most unjustly. The Nazis labelled Sinti and Roma as a 'social problem' that 'poisoned' their Aryan Master-race, so they murdered over half a million of them in the Holocaust. Many people all over Europe still consider Roma and Travellers a 'social nuisance' that spoils their community. Local councillors are certainly not Nazis but they sometimes fail to treat Travellers as people - people for whom it is part of their responsibility to provide for as much as for anyone else.

After all the 'common land' had been enclosed, Travellers depended on farmers and other landowners to allow them onto their land. This was usually to do with the Travellers working for them and everyone was pretty much satisfied. More and more of the work Travellers were used to doing became industrialised in factories. Travellers were not used to working indoors and factory managers were reluctant to employ them anyway. It became an increasing problem for the Travellers to find anywhere to park their caravans that was not immediately declared 'illegal' and police called to chase them off. With nothing else available to them, they had to pitch on roadside verges and public parkland. Understandably, this led to increased hostility between the Travellers and the local communities they were part of. Travellers, like most families, are house-proud and family oriented; their main concern is to raise their children and always have enough food for them. When constantly attacked, kept out of local meeting places such as pubs, harassed when trying to access health and education services and unable to find employment, some of the them took to dubious and even criminal activities simply to survive. Some local councils began to make efforts to create legal sites for their Travellers but many didn't.

Instead of consulting with the Travellers' leaders, these local councils just drove them on to become a problem elsewhere and complained to the government to make laws to resolve the problem. On the whole people, even young children, don't respond well to being told what to do by authorities. They are more likely to co-operate if they are invited to take part in planning the solution to the problem. In those boroughs where this didn't happen, the problem has simply got worse. Travellers, who had been content to travel in small groups, started travelling or meeting in much larger groups for protection and local people felt threatened by this.

Hostility increased and some councils started forcing

Travellers to live in council housing. This usually proved a dismal failure. Many Travellers have a phobia about living in 'bricks and mortar' houses instead of 'on wheels'. And the neighbours were usually unwilling to accept Travellers coming to live next door.

Such was the mood of complaints all round, that Prime Minister John Major advised Travellers to buy their own land. This might have resolved the problem if Planning Laws had been used wisely, as they were by some borough councils, to provide for the Travellers in their local communities. But many boroughs refused planning permission for Travellers to live on the land they bought. Planning Law gives councils the right to refuse applications for permanent living quarters and it was often interpreted to the council's liking and to the disadvantage of Travellers. People who are prejudiced against Travellers put a lot of pressure on their local council to keep the Travellers out.

I am often asked how I would like it if a lot of Travellers settled on a plot next to my home. My answer is to treat them with respect as people. I would go to them in friendship with a pot of tea and a tray of cakes. If they accepted my friendship, I would welcome them. If they turned nasty on me, I would call the police. But I would give them a chance first. The problem usually starts with local people making aggressive instead of friendly approaches to start with.

Travellers are usually peace-loving and friendly if they feel accepted and respected. How would you feel if, on moving into a new home, the neighbours looked down on you and made you feel unwelcome?

THE STORY OF DALE FARM

About 30 years ago a group of Travellers bought a field called Dale Farm, in the borough of Basildon. At that time Basildon Council had put down a concrete base in order to use part of the field as a junk-yard for outworn heavy vehicles. The Council did not object to the Travellers buying the field from the owner and clearing the junk-yard at their own expense. A few families received planning permission to install chalets to live there permanently. Because of the scarcity of legal places for Travellers, more and more came to Dale Farm. The local 'settled' community complained strongly and no more planning permission was granted. A new council was voted in over ten years ago on a promise to get rid of the Travellers. The new Chairman of Basildon Council announced in the local paper that he would rid the borough of Travellers. A ten-year battle then ensued between Basildon Council and the Dale Farm Travellers plus their growing number of supporters. With the backing of the International and other Roma organisations and the support of many non-Roma organisations and individuals, the Dale Farm Travellers won many injunctions against Basildon Council, which prevented the council evicting them. But Basildon Council could afford more highly skilled lawyers and finally got the court permission and Tony Ball, as Chair of the Council, finally presided over the horrific eviction on October 18th 2011.

The ten-year legal battle between the Travellers and the council was extremely complicated and hard for anyone but lawyers to understand. But the lawyers could only use the existing law and Planning Law gives Basildon Council the right to evict Travellers, if they are living without planning permission, even if they own the land. Repeatedly the judges stressed the humanitarian issues. Among these were that Basildon should make provision of culturally adequate accommodation (as compared to unacceptable council housing) for those made homeless by eviction; that vulnerable elderly, sick and young children must not be exposed to trauma and physical damage, and that legal property be respected. This was virtually impossible to carry out, as Basildon brought in 150 riot police with stun guns to break into the Dale Farm compound and arrest or chase away the token resistance of activists, ahead of the bailiffs. The bailiffs smashed a lot of protected property bringing in their heavy machinery to smash everything that had not been taken off the site, set fire to it and then bulldoze a wall of earth round the

Eviction of site near Basildon

Dale Farm before Eviction

Dale Farm after Eviction

site to stop the Travellers going back on it. This, of course, deprives them of their legal right to graze horses and sheep on the land they own.

This brutal invasion by the police probably would not have been possible for Basildon without the substantial subsidy from the government of around £6 million. The total cost of the eviction itself, including over 10 years of legal fees was around £18 million. This huge sum of money has not resolved anything and has in fact been wasted. The Travellers are still there. As most of them have nowhere to go, they are parked all along the side of the lane leading to the blocked Dale Farm entrance. Without water or sanitation this is a health hazard that could lead to an epidemic. The saddest aspect of the whole thing is that eviction was totally unnecessary. The Land Agency found some land that the Travellers were prepared to accept in exchange for Dale Farm, but Basildon Council refused this. From the filming of the eviction, which hit the national news on TV, and was also viewed in many other countries, the 'over-kill' and brutality of it looked rather like retribution against the Travellers for the repeated temporary injunctions they won in the court processes.

The story of Dale Farm was far from ended by the eviction. Court cases continue with claims against Basildon Council over the damage to persons and property during the eviction. Basildon claimed that the eviction was necessary to restore Dale Farm to 'greenbelt'. But the eviction left it as a wall of bulldozed earth round a pool and quagmire in the middle. The TV coverage brought the horror that the Dale Farm Travellers suffered to almost everyone's notice. It got people talking about it and voicing their prejudices. Once prejudice is out in the open it can be challenged. People who have grossly misunderstood can be given accurate information and encouraged to think and ask questions before jumping to prejudiced conclusions. Many people simply don't realise that they have prejudiced images in their minds of Travellers based on hearsay, 'old wives tales' and wrong information. Again and again, I have heard people say, "I am not racist but the Travellers have only themselves to blame". It is hard for people to learn that what they thought was true turns out to be prejudice, and that they colluded with heaping unreasonable blame on Travellers. Many people who saw the eviction on the national TV news started questioning: what sort of society we are to let people be treated so brutally when they have committed no crime other than to be living without planning permission and with nowhere to live legally?

CHAPTER 6

WHERE DO ROMA, TRAVELLERS

AND JEWS LIVE?

BOTH JEWS AND Roma were driven out of their original homelands. The Roma were driven out of Northern India, to become a wandering people. They were considered the most inferior strata of society and were unwanted by everyone. Many of them were taken away as slaves and, as they bore children fathered by their white slave masters, their skin colour became gradually lighter. Some of them have remained quite dark-skinned. Roma have migrated to all countries of the world but, sadly, they are harassed, persecuted and treated unjustly everywhere, particularly badly in Europe. A lot of people have not yet understood that Human Rights are indivisible and labour under the misconception that Human Rights simply don't apply to Roma. In Britain, some people even want a Bill of British Rights that would give more rights to some people than others. If this were to become law, it would really mean the end of democracy. Democracy by definition aims to give everybody equal rights.

Jews, too, were persecuted and treated unfairly over the centuries in most countries of the world. The Jews were originally a wandering people until they settled in Canaan in biblical times. In the year 70AD, the Romans conquered Jerusalem, destroyed the Jewish temple and drove the Jews out to become again a wandering people. They formed Jewish communities that became known as the Diaspora, in just about every country in the world. They took their religion with them and, unlike the Roma, maintained it in the face of pressures to convert. Part of their religion was to keep alive the idea of returning to their homeland in Palestine. Jews tend to live in the past and the future. The bible and their history are very important to them and they long and pray for a peaceful future. Roma, on the other hand, live much more in the present. Savouring the present moment is more important to them than the past and the future. But their past and their future are as important for the total community as yours and mine. Instead of discounting or ignoring them, it would benefit all of us to learn more about Roma and Travellers as well as Jews.

Since 1971 and the creation of the Roma Union, Roma and Travellers see themselves now as a Roma Nation – a nation without a homeland. Some people who are not Roma, have suggested a homeland for them in part of India. Roma have expressed no wish for this. Unlike Jews, they have no wish to go back to their original homelands, they consider themselves and are European as they have been in Europe over 500 years. They simply want to be accepted as Europeans.

Jews, from the time they were driven out of Palestine, always cherished the hope of returning. The Roma simply want to be accepted as equals in the countries in which they live, and in which most of them are citizens.

There is a powerful myth about Roma that they both disdain and wantonly break every law they please and that the law is unfairly in their favour and against the settled community. People who believe this myth are naturally furious, feel cheated and angry and become increasingly hostile towards Travellers and Roma, who they perceive as having the power and influence to flout the law, take over the area and spoil everything for those who were there before them. Few people are aware that Roma have been part of the European community, including Britain of course, for at least five hundred years, probably more. They used to be an important part of our economy as seasonal agricultural workers and skilled craftspeople. Our laws have enclosed and taken away all the 'common land' where they formerly pitched in their travels. Their former livelihood has been almost totally mechanised and they are largely excluded socially and economically.

In Britain two thirds of the roughly 300,000 Roma and Travellers live in ordinary housing, integrated and largely 'invisible' in the community. The myth focuses on the approximately 100,000 (out of a UK population of about sixty-three million) Travellers who want to continue their traditional life style 'on wheels' instead of in 'bricks and mortar' houses. Most of these are itinerant Travellers who want a permanent base (a large family chalet caravan) and space to park a car and trailer-caravan. This is not so different to the main population who want a brick house with space to park a car and trailer/boat/etc. Perhaps the crucial difference is that we are three generations past the extended family structure. We are used to living in nuclear families or other small households, often distant from our relatives. Roma and Travellers are family-oriented and want to live together in groups of families called Kumpania. So they need groups of pitches close together. This is also to do with protection against racist persecution and constant attacks and fear of attack. Settled communities become very frightened of a large and increasing community of itinerant Travellers. In reality the Travellers are just as frightened of the settled community. As soon as a few Travellers arrive in a locality, everything that goes missing is blamed on Traveller thieves and everything that goes wrong must be their fault too, just like the Nazis blamed everything bad, however absurd, on 'the Jews'.

The local settled community tends then to protest against the Travellers being given planning permission even when they buy land, which a previous government recommended they do. The laws relating to accommodation and services for Travellers are complex and difficult to understand, involving tortuous clauses that have been modified and changed many times. Far from favouring Travellers, as so many people think, they are heavily stacked against Gypsies. The government, for all its slogan "Every Child Matters", has dismally failed to educate Traveller children to a standard that enables them to claim a voice in the democratic process. If they do not have a 'legal' address they have no vote even if they were able to claim it. There is very little real consultation with the Roma and Traveller communities. Local councils, mostly made up of people who know little and care less about the plight of Travellers, tend to bow to the protests of their most vociferous anti-Gypsy protesters in order to secure votes.

The problem centres on a shortage of about 3000 legal pitches for itinerant Travellers and the government allocated £60 million for local authorities to claim from to help them provide new pitches. Local authorities are responsible for assessing the needs of Roma and Travellers in their borough and providing for them. Some boroughs, such as Newham and Durham, have taken their responsibility seriously. But others, instead of applying for the government money to provide the necessary pitches, decide that Travellers are not part of their community and determine to drive them out of the borough into nowhere. Evicted Travellers, who have nowhere that is legal to go, have to pitch somewhere illegally. Then they really are a nuisance. Repeated eviction traumatises them and makes them angry, suspicious and uncooperative. Travellers are accused of leaving a mess of rubbish behind; but would you bag up your rubbish and take it with you if you were woken at 5am by police and given 20 minutes to get out? If your local council wants to requisition your home, perhaps to widen the road, they are legally obliged to give you compensation or a similar home elsewhere. But Travellers are brutally evicted from land they own by some local councils who take away their land without compensation as charges for the cost of the eviction!

Both Jews and Roma have traditional rituals for both religion and ordinary living. While the Jewish ones are written in details in their books, the Roma ones, are passed from parents to children by word and in stories that are told round the camp fire or in family gatherings. Part of the Roma tradition, called 'Romanipen' is that some of the rituals must never be told to any non-Roma as that might result in bad luck of some sort. Of course this means the rituals cannot be written down. Also, as most Roma have suffered a lot of harassment, they tend to be rather suspicious of people until they get to know them well. This means they usually keep their story-telling private.

Both Jews and Roma have their own national anthem. The Roma national anthem, "Gelem Gelem", is the youngest.

Composed by Serbian-born Zarko Janovic, a talented balalaika player after WWII, it was chosen in 1971 at the inauguration of the Roma Nation and made official at the 4th Congress of Roma in 2004. The Jewish national anthem, "Ha 'Tikvah" was composed by Naphtali Herz Imber of Galicia in 1886 and adopted by the State of Israel in 1948. The British national anthem, "God save our gracious Queen/King" is even older. It goes back at least to 1745 when the lyrics were first published in Gentleman's Magazine. It is thought to be composed by Henry Purcell around 1650 with lyrics by John Bull. The full lyrics of all three anthems are given in the Index.

Persecution of Gypsies and Jews, and the misery both groups have suffered over centuries, is shameful for humanity. Nevertheless, these two groups have survived against the odds. They have had to develop resilience and adaptability. That is why they have been able to survive when many ethnic groups have died out. Survival of the fittest, in the true Darwinian sense, means to adapt and survive or fail to adapt and disappear. For Gypsies and Jews, adaptation has been at a huge personal and collective cost; and yet both groups have remained positive and vibrant. They have both given so much to it in spite of receiving so much rejection from humanity. Both groups have a love of music and entertainment and their own flavour of humour. They have given us Gypsy music and Kletzmer, Story-telling and Hollywood films.

Although anti-Semitism and Anti-Gypsyism, seem to be on the rise, the truth is that they have always been there. Sometimes they die down, only to rise up again in times of anxiety and stress. Stereotyped images in the mind, fear and envy of others who appear very different and scapegoating are part of being human. We can't get rid of them but we can learn to keep the feelings and desires to ourselves without actively taking them out on other people. We can learn to respect and treat all people equally if we have the courage and will to do so. And there are signs of progress. Since the end of WWII, Roma and Travellers have been getting more education, which enables them to begin claiming their rightful voice. They have been coming together and forming organisations, both local and international, for protection and to protest their unfair treatment. The Roma Virtual Network was created 19th July 1999 and now provides information and links between individuals and organisations. Jews have always had education and organisations and now they are starting to support the Roma efforts to catch up. Two Jewish organisations, Rene Cassin and Aegis have created projects to raise awareness and challenge stereotypes and prejudice against Roma. The Nazi genocide against Sinti and Roma is increasingly more often included in both Holocaust education and Holocaust commemoration.

Prejudice and persecution of Gypsies is most intense in Eastern European countries, Hungary, Slovakia, Romania and the Czech Republic in particular. Because of this, here have been mass migrations of Roma Westwards in Europe and also to Canada and Norway. These countries, on the whole, try to stop them coming, deport them back or make unfair restrictions to try and control them. These measures are mostly counterproductive. The solution can only be through raising awareness, changing prejudiced attitudes and treating them with dignity and fairness. If we want to have Human Rights ourselves we have to accept the responsibility that goes along with those Rights – to make sure all people have the same Rights.

CHAPTER 7

STORIES

LIKE EVERY ETHNIC-CULTURAL group, Jews and Romany groups have their special stories. Children love to hear stories and they not only enjoy them but also learn from them about the world they live in and the people in it. Even if it is not quite so exciting, it is safer and still enjoyable to experience action at second hand by watching or listening to stories. Adults like stories too because inside every adult there is still the child they once were, and adults learn from stories too. So stories are immensely important.

Most Jews grow up with books as Jewish homes usually have bookcases full of books of one sort or another. So it is not surprising that a large number of Jews have written books about their personal stories and experiences, and the legends that were formerly handed down verbally. A lot of Roma have grown up either in caravans and vardos or in very poor housing conditions where there is no room for bookcases. Until quite recently most Roma and Travellers have not been interested in books or reading and writing. They are primarily skilled in crafts and various forms of art and music, so they are used to communicating with sounds and movements rather than the written words. But they are also famous for story-telling. They have no lack of imagination when it comes to story-telling, which they tend to do with a lot of drama that is gripping.

At an international Jewish youth camp in Berlin in July 2013, where I had been invited to speak about the Kindertransport, there was a Russian youth leader who told stories. The children adored her and couldn't get enough of her stories because she didn't just tell them, she enacted them. I too was gripped by her stories even though I could not understand a word of them. Although Dasha is a Jew, I was not surprised to find out that she has a Romany grandfather and is very proud of him. She told me that she doesn't usually tell people because she doesn't want anti-Gypsy people to insult him. She was pleased to give me permission to include her in this book and she later sent me a photo of her grandfather.

It took a long time after the Holocaust before Jewish survivors were willing and able to give their testimonies. Some of them wanted to talk about their experiences much sooner but they were not believed and sometimes were told they must be exaggerating or mentally deranged. Personal stories are very precious and if a person feels unheard or discounted they clam up and may never be able to try again. Only when you have a listener who you know really wants to hear your story, and will not make you feel uneasy or embarrassed, can you tell it as it really was. Even then, sometimes you start remembering things you didn't even know you had forgotten. That can be painful, too. Learning about the Holocaust has been a required topic in the national curriculum in England since 1991. The Holocaust Education trust and other organisations have encouraged survivors to tell their stories to groups of students in schools and colleges, and many of them have written books too.

Roma and Travellers tend to be reluctant to tell their life stories or give their testimonies to researchers. Many feel that they will only be laughed at. How can they be expected to trust anybody when they are still being treated badly and insulting things said about them, especially in the press? There is a myth that Roma and Travellers are unable to learn to read and write so that they can't write books. In fact there are lots of books written by Roma and Travellers, and about them, if you take the trouble to look for them. Some suggestions are listed in the appendix. A growing number of Roma have written really interesting books about their childhood memories and some have written about their experiences in the Nazi concentration camps; hopefully, more will do so. To add to the problem, it is rather hard for them to get a publisher willing to take on their books. Some publishers think that not many people want to read about Gypsies and fear they won't make enough money selling such books. Jews have developed much further and there are quite a few Jewish publishers that specialise in Jewish books. Now that they have an international organisation as well as many local ones in different countries, the Roma are beginning to catch up.

Since the inauguration of the annual Holocaust Memorial Day on January 7th 2001, there has been an explosion of excellent information and teaching material about the Holocaust. Packs and websites offering a vast range of materials for study can be contacted through the various Holocaust education organisations listed in the Appendix. This material refers to many books written by and about Jews but offers little, as yet, about Roma and Travellers. Therefore the Appendix gives a list of books about them.

PERSONAL STORIES

Many Jews have written books or given interviews about their personal experiences, but it has taken about 50 years after the Holocaust before they were able to include their experiences of this atrocity. It takes a long time after the trauma has stopped externally, to do enough repairs to the damage it has done inside, before a person can talk or write publicly about it. For most Roma, the trauma has not yet stopped. Some have assimilated into the community and are fearful of being identified as Gypsies. Most are still being traumatized by attacks, insults and other humiliation by people who are mostly ignorant about their culture. So their stories need to be told by others until they are ready to tell them themselves. We particularly need to hear success stories in the media to counter the negative and insulting reportage about Gypsies. Ramona's story is one such success story that was reported in a local newspaper.

RAMONA

Ramona, a Romani Gypsy from Romania, came to England aged 27, as many Romanian Roma do to escape the awful conditions they suffer in Romania. She had no formal education and spoke little English before she came. So she sold The Big Issue for 18 months outside Manchester Central Library and, when it closed for refurbishment, she continued in Rochdale town centre and focused on learning English. As she became fluent in English she was invited to take part in a pioneering training scheme for Young Roma run by the City Council and partners. She went on to work as a community interpreter, youth and family worker and classroom assistant. Because of her rapid achievements she was selected for an invitation to a Jubilee lunch at Manchester town hall, attended by the Queen and Prince Philip.

PAPUSZA

Bronislawa Wajs, born in Poland in 1908 was affectionately known as Papusza. She had a very unhappy marriage with a much older man. During the horrors of war she found some solace in writing poetry and singing. After WWII she became one of the most famous Polish poets. An American author, Colum McCann wrote a novel about a Slovak Romani woman he called Marienks Novotna with a nick-name Zoli. It was clearly the story of Papusza. Now a film is being made of Papusza's life.

Sally, Yvonne and Robin are three Romanies who are ready and willing to share their stories with you. All three of them have lived through hardships and insults but have come through with determination to do what they can to help others still struggling. They are thee very positive stories. I suspect there are many more like them but either they have not yet been voiced or they have been little noticed.

SALLY'S STORY

I am the British Romani Gypsy you can see in the short film "Porrajmos" that Plymouth and Devon Racial Equality Council made for schools to show a bit of our Romani culture and our ancestors who were murdered in the Nazi Holocaust. I live in Devon, quite near where I was born, but in my own chalet caravan. It looks like a bungalow house but it has wheels, which you can't see. I lived in a house (without wheels) on two occasions in my life and each time I became very depressed. This was partly because it was more difficult for my family and friends to visit me when I lived in a house. An important part of our culture is that family come in their caravans and stay for a while and then move on again. Family is very important to us; even though we are scattered all over the country, I am in touch with nearly all my family on my father's side and in contact with some of my mother's sisters.

My Great-grandfather, William, bought a piece of land in the middle of the village of Westlake, near Plymouth and was fully accepted there. He had thirteen children and, when they had their own families, they lived on the land. My granddad Charley married one of Williams's daughters, Flory, and bought the land opposite and lived there for many years with my Dad, his brothers and their families. I was born in a nearby hospital while my parents lived there, but when I was three years old my parents emigrated to Australia with my older brother and sister and me. I actually had my third birthday on the plane going there. Lots of British Romanies went to Australia because there is more space there to travel around than in Britain and people are not so prejudiced there.

My Dad's family are Romanies going back many generations. My Mum was not Romani but what, in our culture, we call Gorjies (or Gadje), which simply means 'not Romani'. We have a Romani language, Romanes, but we tend to speak mainly English with some Romani words and phrases mixed in. I am very proud of our culture, which has very high standards and strict rules about cleanliness and high morals; so it is very stupid as well as insulting when people who don't know us call us 'dirty Gypsies'.

We came back to England after about a year because my Dad was ill with asthma and wanted to be near his family; I think he was homesick. We went out to Australia again when I was about six and my younger brother was born there. We came back to Devon when I was 8 and I didn't go to school any more after that but I taught myself till I could read well and write too and use the computer. I want my own children to go right through secondary school and get good jobs. Most Romani parents are suspicious of secondary school as they fear that their children will be affected by the lower standards and morals of some of the other children and will no longer value their Romani culture.

We went back a third time to Australia and I used to go out painting and decorating with my Dad and older siblings. I came back on my own when I was seventeen. I fell out with my parents, as so many strong-willed teenagers do when they want to be independent. My parents were never satisfied with what I did, especially the cleaning. They continued to live in Australia but have recently returned to live in the UK. My two brothers are in England but my sister, Louise who I am very close to, still lives in Australia and travels with her husband and two grown-up children.

When I came back to England on my own I got jobs in several factories and in one of them, an aerosol factory, I met my husband. He was the manager, and is a Gorje not a Romany Gypsy. I was driving a fork-lift there. Nowadays most Romani Gypsies don't have arranged marriages. They usually meet each other at parties and other people's weddings – and they don't have the sort of weddings that Channel 4 think they have. I have never been to such a wedding and I have been to a lot. The Channel 4 dressmaker, Thelma, is not a Gypsy, neither a Romani nor an Irish Traveller, but seems to think she knows all about the Traveller and Gypsy community; but I don't think she knows anything much about us otherwise she would not work with channel 4 making herself and her customers look ridiculous. I think she caters for a small minority of Gypsies and this does not represent the entire Gypsy and Traveller Community.

I married my husband in Gretna Green and he is the only partner I have had. My parents were in Australia and only his father came to our wedding as his mother was ill. We have a daughter aged eight and a son aged seven and another baby is on the way. I think three will be enough as this one will be a Caesarian like the older two. I am employed by the Government Communities Department part time, with two councillors, to run a three hour course for councillors in different boroughs to help them understand the needs of the Gypsies in their boroughs. I like my work because I think it is important for Gypsies and Gorje to understand each other.

YVONNE'S STORY

I lost my grandfather and an uncle in the Holocaust. My uncle Freddie was killed at age 15 by the Nazis in the gas chamber. We always light a candle on August 2nd for Remembrance Day for the Romani victims of the Holocaust because on the night of August 1st 1944, 4000 of our fellow Romanies were murdered in Auschwitz. We'll always remember them.

I have two brothers. They live in Germany and they never married. We are not in touch any more since me and my family moved to Australia. My Mum, she's still alive and on medication for depression and for her nerves. My Dad, he's a Gadjo (not a Romani). He used to be a part time priest for 20 years. He also worked in Bosch where my Mum met him, as he was her supervisor. I still remember as a kid walking in the forest with my Sinti grandmother and her pointing out old vardos scattered all around the area. She told me that these empty wooden vardos of the Sinti and Roma were now used by German forestry workers to have their lunch and tea breaks. Yet another sad reminder of the atrocities and crimes that happened to our people!

I also remember when my grandmother took me to the farm where they didn't mind us touching and feeding the horses once in a while. We gave the horses brown sugar cubes and apples and my grandmother showed me how to touch them, and it was great. I loved the horses and have since ridden on horses and so have my kids, but it is expensive so we don't get to do it much. My Sinti grandmother was born on January 8th 1902 and would be 110 if she were alive. She is alive in my heart inspiring me to fight for justice. It's hard and I often feel like I'm banging my head against a brick wall. There is so much prejudice, but I carry on just trying to break down the stereotypes, which are harming our culture so much.

I left Germany at 18 because I could not stand to live there any more. I chose to come to the UK and lived 12 years in London. My Australian husband, who had worked 12 years in Britain, was refused renewal of his work permit. So we went back to Germany and I wrote my book *Torn Away Forever* while we were there. But the racism was so bad that we left Europe and went to Brisbane, Australia in 2004. We ran a Romani café in Melbourne for a while. But racism got so bad we moved to Adelaide, where my children went to a Romani school. When the school closed we moved to Cairns in North Queensland where we worked with the director of a local historical museum to put on a display of Romani culture. Then we were invited to Perth to work with a Romani man to start a Romani school. This proved a disappointment, as the Romani community there were not very interested.

My kids are proud and protective towards their Romani heritage, and proud of their identity. Eve is 10 and has spoken about our Romani roots and culture in front of her whole class in two schools. In one class she got an award for the most interesting news. She took part in a multicultural photo contest run by the Queensland government.

My son, Tim who is 12, did a project once at school called "Project India". You had to mention a country and he tied it in with our Romani culture and our history coming from India. He made it colourful with pictures of food, language samples and maps. He got an A for it from the teacher. Unfortunately, in the same school a bit later he got picked on and called names and teased because of his Romani heritage. In the next school, he spoke up even louder and more when they wrote the word Gypsy with a small 'g'. They said it was a 'world word' and that we didn't exist! So we educated the whole school, but never really became friends with any of them. We were always the 'outsider', but they wouldn't do wrong to us any more at least.

My youngest son, Ben, he's seven and has a sensitive nature. He hates it when teachers shout. He is good at school, but hasn't got very clear speech, which he needs out there, so he often won't talk at all to strangers. He's shy and keeps close to his family.

Now we are leaving Coffs Harbour and going to Brisbane, back in Queensland. I have a friend. She's a Romani from Scotland and now lives in the North of Brisbane. We hope to do Romani events and work together.

I am part of an international team of Romani Rights advocates educating the Australian public about our Romani culture. I make long journeys across this vast country to set up Romani exhibitions. I give interviews on radio and speak about our culture in primary schools. We have survived for 1000 years; time is on our side, we are still here, but we can't sit and rest. We must keep educating the public in any way we can.

ROBIN'S STORY

I have both Jewish and Gypsy ancestry: Jewish on my mother's side and Gypsy on my father's side. There is a possibility of added Jewish Sephardic ancestry on my father's in the form of an Italian Jewish Dentist in Edinburgh, but DNA evidence would be needed to be sure.

My maternal grandparents came from Bessarabia and the Ukraine. Bessarabia, meaning house of the Arabs, was at one time part of the Ottoman Empire, then part of Romania or Moldavia. My Grandfather's birthplace was a Shtetl, or Jewish settlement, which was too small to have a name. It was shared in winter by the local Gypsies. Its location, somewhere near Kallis was at various times described as being in Russia, Ukraine, Romania Moldavia and Transnistria. After emigrating, my grandfather lived in England but was legally stateless.

There were cultural ties between Jews and Gypsies in the Stetl, especially reflected in their music. To some extent their lifestyles and economic life also converged. My grandfather often described himself humorously as the last of the wandering Jews. Despite being a taboo in both camps intermarriage, and interbreeding did occur. The extended family includes a potter called Erik Stokl, born in Austria just before the war, who is Jewish and Gypsy. More distantly related was Louis Freiber, a Klezmer violinist who played in the Quintet De Hot Club De Paris with the famous Django Reinhart. Not related but apparently sharing similar mixed ancestry were Charley Chaplin and Michael Caine.

My father, Horace Clelland Jamieson, was the son of Scottish Gypsies from around Hamilton in Lanark. His parents John and Hannah Jamieson were similar to Irish Travellers in their lifestyle but their religion was Church of Scotland rather than Roman Catholic. They spoke English interspersed with a few words of Romanes, which comes from Sanskrit, in much the same way as many of the English Gypsies. Some Romanes word they used are mush or mushie, parni, gorgie, and chore, but they spoke them with a strong Scottish accent.

There are Gypsy Jamiesons in the highlands and many more around Dundee. They seem to have a shared culture, which defines them as highly intelligent petty criminals, and my family has to some extent distanced itself from Gypsy culture in an effort to get the children educated. I am the first in this line who has not been imprisoned. My father served two sentences and my grandfather at least five for seemingly pointless offences. (Perhaps criminality needs to be studied by anthropologists in relation to Gypsy and Traveller culture, rather than politely ignored or dismissed as a consequence of poverty).

Although I am a Chartered Psychologist and an Associate Fellow of the British Psychological Society, I have always had a van or caravan and like to move around most of the time, either alone or staying near friends and family. I have tried living in houses but never adapted, or lost the feeling of being trapped, not free to go, unable to trust the structure of bricks and mortar. I have also tried staying on campsites but found them too regimented and similar to an open prison.

I was for many years the District Psychologist, then Head of Psychology, Psychotherapy and Art Therapy for an NHS Trust in Essex, based at Runwell Hospital near Wickford, Essex. I specialised in Personal construct theory and applied psychophysiology, which in combination lend themselves to application in a cross cultural context. Using these methods I was able to offer a service to some Gypsies and Travellers who often do not benefit from conventional psychological services.

My main home for the last 15 years has been a green Mercedes Sprinter van which I converted myself as a motor caravan. It has been designed as a 'wild camper' with windows on the nearside only so that parked near a wall it looks like a delivery vehicle and attracts less attention from the police. I have travelled in the van to all parts of the UK and Eire, and to all European countries except Russia and the Baltic States. The van is a 1996 model, converted from new. Before that I had a caravan for a while, and a very old Bedford CA van, Romany conversion.

After retiring in 1997 I went abroad for about five years and travelled extensively in Asia and Australia. In Asia I was using public transport and staying mostly in remote rural areas, sleeping in tents, huts and hostels – sometimes even in caves. I was also in Australia for two years with my partner, and we lived in a 1992 Mazda bus converted as a motorhome, but added extra water tanks for a journey across the central desert. We went to remote stations, Rodeos and the camel races. We met indigenous people still living a nomadic lifestyle and found ourselves to be more adventurous and self sufficient than most of the Australians we met. People are not as hostile in Australia to the travelling lifestyle as they are in England. I still write a bit about my travelling lifestyle, using a different name. I have also offered travelling people a limited service as a clinical psychologist. I find that they can speak to me more easily in a van or trailer that they would in an NHS clinic.

These three people have given me their personal permission to tell you their stories in this book. There are an increasing number of personal Roma stories already out in the public domain. I will mention only three that have moved me deeply: Ceija Stojka, Walter Winter and Rosa Mettbach. Details of the books are in the Appendix.

Ceija Stojka was born in 1933 in a Roma family that travelled in the regions around Vienna. She survived Auschwitz and was liberated when she was only 11 with her mother in Bergen-Belsen. She later became a well known writer and wrote a book especially for young children about her liberation from Bergen-Belsen.

Walter Winter was one of nine children in a German Sinto family. He was conscripted into the German Navy but discharged 'on racial grounds' and deported to Auschwitz. He was deported again to Ravensbrueck and then Sachsenhausen and later re-conscripted to fight the Rd Army on the Russian Front.

Rosa Mettbach was one of the few members of her Roma family in Germany to survive by escaping to the USA. There she met and made friends with Toby Sonneman, a Jew. Together they raised enough money for a tour of Europe in which they researched the fate of their two families in the Holocaust. Later Toby wrote the book "Shared Sorrows" describing their friendship and research together.

Six more Sinti and Roma Holocaust stories are available in a digital exhibition on the Internet at www.romasinti.eu:

- Zoni Weisz: a hidden child during the war in Holland, the only survivor from his large family, now famous for flower arrangements for international events.
- Krystina Gil: a Polish girl who escaped from Plaszow concentration camp.
- Elina Machalkova: born in Czechoslovakia, survived forced labour in a concentration camp and later became a famous singer and writer.
- Settela Steinbach: the nine year old German Sinti girl in a white headscarf looking out of a cattle truck in the

Westerbork collection camp in Holland. This picture became an icon of the Holocaust as she was mistaken to be Jewish. She died in Auschwitz.

- Amalie Schaich Reinhardt: German born, sent to Auschwitz and liberated from Bergen Belsen.
- Karl Stojka: arrested in his classroom, deported to Auschwitz, survived three concentration camps and became a well known artist, dies in 2003.

The story of Romani Rose, the son of Romanies murdered in the Holocaust is available on:

www.rromaniconnect.org/Romasintiholocaust.html

Dasha's Gypsy grandfather

Yvonne and family in Australia

The author (left) with Sally giving a talk at a school

Robin with his Mazdabus in Australia

Robin and his family Vardo

CHAPTER 8

RACE, ETHNICITY AND THE HOLOCAUST

AND O PORRAJMOS

THE WORD 'RACE' is widely misunderstood. Because of this it is often misused, and misused in such a way that it perpetuates the misunderstanding. There is only one Human Race. Biologists call the Human Race Homo Sapiens, which is a species of mammals. There have been previous Human Species, the fore-runners of Homo Sapiens, but none of these are alive today, except in science fiction films.

What people call 'races' are inventions or labels, not actual races. Just like you and me, Jews and Roma are all members of the one Human Race. Roma and Jews are two rather different ethnic-cultural groups. We need to go back to biology to understand the difference. Members of a race or species cannot mate with any other race or species and produce fertile offspring. Horses and donkeys are two separate species; they can mate together, but the offspring, mules and hinnies, are infertile. You can't mate two mules together. If you want more mules you have to mate another horse and donkey together. Lygers provide another example. The offspring of a lion and a tiger is called a lyger; but lygers are infertile and can't have babies.

Human beings can't produce babies with any other species, although some weird science fiction stories have been written about chimeras (half human and half something else) such as the ever popular Dr Jekyll and Mr. Hyde. And of course mermaids are a popular part of our cultural collection of fairy tales; but they don't exist in reality. They only exist in myths and fairytales. As Jews and Roma are ethnic-cultural groups, they can intermarry and have children. This happens, but not too often, as their cultures are very different and each group does not like its young people marrying 'outsiders'. If they really trust you, some Romanies will tell you about their Jewish ancestors. I imagine some Jews have Gypsies in their ancestry but I have not been told of any.

Whereas you can never leave the Human Race and join another 'race', you can leave the ethnic-cultural group you were born into if you want to. Lots of people do just this through intermarriage, which is marriage between two people from different ethnic-cultural groups. To use again what we learn from biology, ethnic-cultural groups are like breeds of dogs, cats or horses. To keep the breed 'pure' you must only allow 'pedigree' individuals to mate together. A pedigree is a family tree that proves all the individuals going back several generations have the same features that define the breed. If all pet dogs were released 'into the wild' to interbreed, within a few generations they would revert back to wolves.

NEANDERTHAL MAN — A DIFFERENT RACE OR SPECIES
TO MODERN MAN
HOMO SAPIENS

HORSE

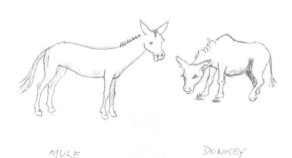

MULE   DONKEY

Non-pedigree pet dogs and cats are often called 'mongrels' and 'moggies', which some pet-owners find insulting, like Roma are insulted by being called 'gypsies'. Two things are interesting about mongrels and moggies. Firstly, when two mongrels or two moggies mate together, their offspring can be very different to both parents. To understand this you need to study genetics. Secondly, mixed breed individuals are usually stronger and fitter than pedigree ones. That is why, if let loose, the mongrels and moggies would probably kill the pedigree individuals or drive them away from food so that they would starve.

The Human Race is composed mainly of 'mongrels'. Throughout history, the conquerors have always raped and/or married the women of the conquered group. This still happens in wars, but also through economic migration and refugee groups seeking asylum, or simply people meeting a partner while travelling on holiday. Attempts by human groups to maintain a 'pedigree blood line' have usually come to grief because of 'weakening' the 'gene-stock' by cousin marriages. An example of this is that the Russian Royal family, which carried the life-threatening disease, haemophilia, in its genes because of so many cousin marriages. Not only aristocratic families but also dictators often want to keep their community 'pure' by preventing them from interacting and breeding with 'outsiders'. In the First World War the Ottoman Turks wanted to purify or 'turkify' Anatolia by forcing all the Christians to convert to Islam and killing those who refused in a horrific genocide. As this was not brought to justice at the end of the war, it provided impunity for more 'ethnic cleansing' and genocide.

In the Second World War Hitler and his Nazi Party decided to create a master-race that would have 'pure blood'. If he had succeeded, his master-race would have been genetically poorer and weaker than the multicultural communities of most countries today. Hitler did not know the work of the Austrian monk and scientist, Gregor Mendel, now recognised as the Father of Genetics. Mendel's theories about inheritance were not recognised until much later. Now you can find out all about his theories and modern genetics on the Internet.

Hitler and those who followed him were convinced that Jews and Roma had bad blood that would poison the pure blood of the Aryan master-race. Hitler also believed in superior and inferior 'races' but he did not invent this idea. The idea of 'white supremacy' was already very strong in Europe and America. Based on Charles Darwin's books *The Origin of Species* and *The descent of Man* in the 19th century,

Sir Francis Galton came up with the idea of Social Darwinism, in England in the late 19th century. By this he meant that the strongest or fittest social groups would survive at the expense of the weaker ones. Hitler built his own theory on this: inferior Slavonic 'races' would support the Aryan master race with slave labour. The most inferior 'races' of Jews and Zigeuner (Roma) were deemed by the Nazis as 'unworthy of life' because they were parasites with poisonous blood and would in the end have to be wiped out.

If only the Social Darwinians of the early 20th century had realised that 'survival of the fittest' is fundamentally based on adaptability to change, not on purity of blood, money, muscle power or the 'gift of the gab'. Because of repeated attacks and persecution, both Roma and Jews have become highly adaptable, with a positive mentality of 'cut your losses and look for a new opening to make something out of nothing'. Roma have been constantly driven away to the edges of communities and have also had to develop skills to adapt and survive under harsh inhospitable conditions. Whereas Jews developed trade and financial skills, Roma developed an outdoor life of camping, depending on 'wheels' to keep on the move and hunting with Lurcher dogs. (See appendix for more about Lurchers.)

At first the Nazis wanted simply to cleanse Germany of the Roma and Jewish impurities by driving them out. Anti-

Jewish and anti-Roma hostility and hatred were very strong all over Europe, not just in Germany. The representatives of 32 countries met in Evian in France in 1938 to discuss the Nazi ill-treatment of Roma and Jews, particularly through the infamous Nuremberg Laws of 1935. Only one country, tiny Dominican Republic, was willing to accept refugees who by that time had been stripped of possessions by the Nazis. All the gates of Europe were slammed shut against them. Once war broke out in September 1939, the Nazis no longer cared what anybody thought. They realised that they could not drive them out so began plans to kill all the Jews and Roma, and anybody else that might oppose them or present any kind of threat. The details of this "final solution", as the Nazis called it, were decided at the Wannsee Conference in Berlin in January 1942.

And so the Nazis set in motion the most horrific, brutal genocide that has ever been. It was meticulously planned and carried out on an industrial scale. What happened was known at the time it was happening; yet no serious measures were taken to stop it. The significance and enormity of this heinous crime was only realised much later and is still being researched after over 70 years. The Holocaust is unique in history but this does not mean it will necessarily remain unique. It has set a precedent, which means that if it has been allowed to happen once, it can happen again. To have a chance of preventing such industrialised murder from being repeated, we all need to learn and think about what actually was done by people to other people, and what people are still doing to other people today.

THE HOLOCAUST AND O PORRAJMOS

The Nazi attempt to wipe out all the Jews and Roma in Europe is called The Shoah (the burden) by Jews and O Porrajmos (the devouring – when Nazi hatred devoured over half a million Roma)) by Roma. It is more generally known as The Holocaust. This word means 'a total sacrifice by fire'. The word was used originally to describe the incident in which the Ottoman Turks locked all the inhabitants of an Armenian village in their church and burnt them alive in it.

Auschwitz is often taken to be a symbol standing for the Holocaust. But it was only one of six concentration camps that were built for the sole purpose of killing the people taken there; and there were over 300 other concentration camps for slave labourers, and even more collection camps for prisoners that had been rounded up awaiting transportation to other camps. That is too much to be held in mind, so Auschwitz, where the greatest number was murdered, has become the symbol standing for all of them.

There was a slave labour camp for Zigeuner (Gypsies) in the village of Lety in Czechoslovakia in the Nazi time, but Czechs ran it not the Nazis themselves. There were many such

Gypsy camps in Moravia and Bohemia too. Many thousands of Gypsies died in these camps from brutal treatment and the last few were sent on to Auschwitz and other camps. The war ended in 1945 but anti-Gypsy hatred continues even today. There is a pig farm now on the site of the Lety camp and the Czech government has so far refused to buy out the farmer and allow a memorial to the murdered Gypsies.

The Nazis murdered a large number of Roma and Sinti in Auschwitz. But also an even larger number of Roma were murdered in Jasenovac, along with Jews. This complex of five concentration camps was built in 1941 – 42 in the independent state of Croatia by the Ustashe Regime. The Croats murdered not only Roma and Jews but also an even greater number of Serbs, who they hated as much as Jews and Roma. And this contributed to the Serbs' attempt to create a pure Serbian 'race' later in the 1990s. Jasenovac was every bit as nasty and brutal as Auschwitz.

There is no room in this book to give a fuller account of the O Porrajmos-Shoah-Holocaust. Hopefully what you have read so far has inspired you to want to find out more and there are some ideas in the Appendix of this book. There are plenty of books and Internet learning materials about the Holocaust that give the story of the Jewish Shoah. Unfortunately, most of these books and other materials barely give the Roma Porrajmos a mention. Roma have only recently started to write books so there are, as yet, rather few books about Porrajmos. They are starting to write to each other from all over the world on email and other social media. You can join the Roma Virtual Network free and get regular emails with up-to-date news from Roma in all countries. All you need to do is to Google "Roma Virtual Network" and you will get a lot of information and emails you can respond to.

The Roma Union has taken August 2nd, the day in 1944 when all the Roma in Auschwitz at the time were liquidated, as the date on which they remember and commemorate the victims of Porrajmos. Jews commemorate Yom HaShoah on the 27th of the Hebrew month of Nisan, as this was chosen by the Israeli government in 1953. As the Hebrew calendar differs from the one we use in Britain, this means some time in April-May. January 27th, the date on which Auschwitz was liberated by the Russian army, was chosen in 2000 by an international task force as an international Holocaust Memorial Day from 2001. Jews and Roma have their separate days to commemorate their murdered ancestors; nevertheless it is important that all other peoples also learn about and mourn the Holocaust, which was a huge loss to the whole of Humanity.

When the Nazis were defeated in 1945 and the camps liberated, the world was horrified to learn how the Jews had been rounded up, brutally treated exploited as slave labour and murdered in gas chambers. There was hardly a mention of the Sinti and Roma Gypsies who went through the same awful experiences. In fact the post-war German government continued to label them as a 'social nuisance', the term the Nazis had used, and refused to regard them as victims of Nazism at all. The German government did not recognise them as victims until 1982, and this came about only when a group of Sinti and Roma invaded Dachau concentration camp and staged a hunger strike there. This forced the government to take notice. Once they were recognised as victims of Nazism, they were able to claim money from the German government to build the Sinti and Roma Documentation and Cultural Centre in Heidelberg in 1987, like Yad Vashem 34 years earlier was enabled by compensation funds for Jews. Many conferences and committee meetings are held in the Heidelberg Centre. It also houses the only permanent exhibition so far of the Nazi genocide against Sinti and Roma. There are permanent exhibitions of the Holocaust all over the world that show the story of the suffering of the Jewish victims but they give very little space if any to the Gypsies who suffered the same fate.

It was some time after the end of the war before commemoration of the Holocaust began. The Holocaust was so horrendous that it was difficult to think about it at all – it was 'unthinkable' that humans could do such awful things to other humans, but we have to face the facts of what people do to other people. All those who survived the war were exhausted and trying to pick up the shattered pieces of their lives. It often takes time before a person is in a fit state to begin thinking and coming to terms with what they went through

Many documentary and feature films about different aspects of the Holocaust were already released in the late 1940s. However, people didn't really start thinking and talking about the Holocaust until the serial programme on TV called "Holocaust" starring Meryl Streep, James Woods and Michael Moriarty was broadcast in 1978. Children who watched this programme, particularly in Germany, asked their parents and teachers whether all this really happened and the adults had to start finding out and thinking about it. The 10 hour film "Shoah" by Claude Lanzmann in 1985 stirred the Jewish communities to realise the full extent of the decimation of their total community. But perhaps it is Spielberg's film "Schindler's List" in 1993 that had the most effect on the general community. Holocaust Education had just been made a requirement in the National Curriculum from September 1991. Teachers, who had no formal education about the Holocaust, were desperate for teaching material. Such material is now in abundance but it was very scarce then. They used "Schindler's list" to evoke reflection and discussion.

I have not been able to find any feature film specifically about Porrajmos before the 1989 Polish film "And the Violins Stopped Playing, directed by Alexander Ramati. Presumably, this was due at least in part to the refusal of the German government to recognise Sinti and Roma as Nazi victims until 1982. Gypsies, all over Europe were simply 'invisible' or when visible considered a 'social nuisance'. They are still regarded as 'socially unwanted' today by many people who lack knowledge and succumb to stereotypes and prejudice. A new feature film to look out for that will tell the story of Porrajmos is "A People Uncounted". It was already released in Canada in 2012.

Memorials for the murdered Jews have been erected in many countries and in all the killing camps and many others. But memorials for the murdered Sinti and Roma are only just beginning. The first major one, in Berlin, was erected in 2013 and you can see photos of it and learn more on www.rromniconnect.org

It seems to have taken popular TV shows again to wake up both the Romani communities and the world to the decimation of the Gypsy communities. The Channel 4 series "My Big Fat Gypsy Wedding" in 2011 seems to have set off something similar to the effects of the TV soap "Holocaust in the 1970s. Whereas "Holocaust" was positive regarding the Jews, the Channel 4 series was deeply insulting to Gypsies. It was supposed to be a documentary to educate the public about the Gypsies and their culture. Instead it was a comedy, aping the film "My Big Fat Greek Wedding", which was made with actors. The Channel 4 programmes, with such a title, invited the public to laugh at Gypsies. People like an opportunity to laugh at someone else's expense. It is called 'schadenfreude'. And of course the popularity of these programmes made a lot of money for Channel 4. However, the programmes raised a massive protest from Roma and Travellers as well as from other knowledgeable and anti-racist people and organisations. Also it, once again, got the school children asking their parents and teachers – is it really like that?

The first world centre for documentation, research, education and commemoration of the Holocaust was created in 1953 in Jerusalem. It was named Yad Vashem, which means 'the hand of God', although many people today consider that God had nothing to do with the Holocaust, which was perpetrated by human beings against other human beings. Lack of concern for others and lack of will to protest about evil deeds, certainly contributed to the Holocaust being allowed to happen.

Beth Shalom, the Holocaust Centre, which opened in September 1995, was the first Holocaust Memorial garden and learning centre in Britain. It was created in Laxton in Nottinghamshire by Stephen and James Smith and their parents, a Christian family who were appalled that post-war born people generally knew little about the Holocaust. But it did not include material about Porrajmos until much later. Now, a branch of the Holocaust Centre called "Aegis" is developing a project about Gypsies.

On 6th June 2000 the Queen opened the only other permanent Holocaust exhibition in England at the Imperial War Museum, London. Both these exhibitions are predominantly about Jews and need to add more acknowledgements of the Roma and Sinti part of the Holocaust. There is as yet no permanent exhibition in this country dedicated to Porrajmos. The one in Heidelberg, Germany is so far the first and only one.

Education about the Holocaust is making enormous progress. It is always linked with learning about Jews as a people before the Holocaust and since. Some educators are beginning to include teaching about the Sinti and Roma before the Holocaust, during it, and afterwards. The Holocaust Education Trust (HET) was established by Lord Grenville Janner and Lord Merlyn Rees in 1988. It was through HET that Holocaust Education was put in the National Curriculum in 1991 so that every student in every school would learn about it. HET also sends educators and Holocaust survivors into schools, takes sixth formers to Auschwitz in its Lessons From Auschwitz project and takes 20 teachers per year to study in Yad Vashem. Several other organisations send speakers into schools and provide educational material and experiences: The London Jewish Cultural Centre, the Anne Frank Trust, The Jewish Museum and others.

Education has been slower to develop about the Roma part of the Holocaust and the Romanies as a people before and since. Until recently, there has been a strange reluctance to acknowledge Roma as a people that should be known about as part of our community. Many people, whose eyes, minds and hearts have not yet opened to the distress caused by ignorance and prejudice, still dismiss them as 'Gypsies' and 'not worth bothering about'.

The first film I came across, made for schools, that focused on the murder of Sinti and Roma in the Holocaust is "Porrajmos", a 15 minute DVD produced by Plymouth & Devon Racial Equality Council in 2012. Sally, who has told you her story in a previous chapter, figures in this DVD. Details are in the Appendix.

Representatives of 44 countries met as an international task force in Stockholm and created January 27th as the International Holocaust Memorial Day. It was chosen as the date the Russian army liberated Auschwitz concentration camp. The first four annual HMD events in Britain were organised by the government and then the task was handed over to a charity, the HMD Trust (HMDT). You can look up the statement the 44 countries signed up to and the aims of the HMDT on the Internet. HMDT is now organising a team in each area of Britain to develop an HMD programme each year to involve as many local people, especially school students.

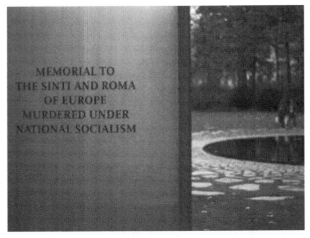

Germany's Sinti-Roma Holocaust Memorial

CHAPTER 9

DENIAL

THE HUMAN MIND is perhaps the most amazing part of our human make-up. It helps us and protects us in so many ways, so that we can get the best out of being alive. We need to treat it with care, because it is a delicate and irreplaceable organ. We have the capacity to imagine ahead what the consequences might be before we act. We have the ability to store enormous amounts of experiences, thoughts and ideas out of the way but ready to be recalled, like files on myriads of shelves. We also have the ability to shut away what we don't want to think about in the 'attic' of our mind, so that we don't even know that we know it. Sometimes, when a person says they don't know something that you can prove they must know, they are not lying but have locked that knowledge away beyond the shelves of files, so that it can't be recalled. Psychologists have shown that we are only conscious or aware of a small portion of the activity of our brain and mind at any one time. If we had all of it in our conscious mind, it would blow like an overloaded electrical circuit.

People who experience a massive trauma, something so awful that they can't deal with it, can cut it out of mind and lock it away. Sometimes they can recall it later, when they feel safe and secure enough, and deal with it then. For many of those who survived the Nazi persecution, including the concentration camps, it was a massive trauma that changed their lives. Only some of them were able to recall and come to terms with the trauma they had suffered. When the genocide, is denied, it is even harder for the traumatised sufferers to come to terms with it. It makes them deeply insecure and unsure of themselves, like losing their 'self' and being unsure they exist. To commit genocide, to be a perpetrator, is also traumatising. The knowledge that you have murdered human people is difficult to deal with because you have broken a very deeply ingrained taboo against killing your own species. So, in order to not think about it you may put it so far 'out of mind' that you can't recall it and can convince yourself it never happened. Or, if it persists in coming back into your mind you can cut off all the feelings connected with it and pretend it away. That is what genocidaires, the perpetrators of genocide, do. They are usually unwilling to take responsibility for the crime they committed. They try to cover it up by getting rid of or hiding the evidence. If they can't do that, they try to blame it on someone else by denial that they had anything to do with it. By continuing to deny what they have done they come to believe that they did not do it. It may take a long time, but the truth usually comes to light in the end.

Until the killing sites are known, the graves identified, memorials established and the trauma of the survivors recognised with some form of reparation, there can be no closure, or ending of the genocide. The genocide continues in a stage of denial. The offspring of the survivors experience the failure of closure through denial like a second murder of their ancestors. They feel it as an attempt to wipe their ancestors out of history, which indeed it is. The unacknowledged trauma also affects the perpetrators; they too can have no closure until they admit and own what they did. Their offspring are then burdened with the shame of the crime and unable to be proud of their ancestors. That is why exposing denial and bearing to face the truth is important. Also, wen genocide is denied and not brought to closure, it creates impunity for more genocide. Once something has been allowed to happen once, it sets a precedent. That means it can happen again. The Holocaust is unique in that it was a deliberately and effectively planned programme of industrialised killing of a selected target group – Gypsies and Jews. But it is only unique so far. Of course it can happen again if there are not enough people with the courage to care and the will to act to prevent it happening again.

As the philosopher Edmund Burke said – For evil to flourish it only needs good men to do nothing.

If you look up Genocide Watch, a website created by Greg Stanton, you will find he has analysed every genocide that has happened. He has shown that every genocide goes through six clearly distinguishable stages before the mass killing begins. This is the time, in these six stages, when we could stop genocide in its tracks if we have the will to do so. History has shown that in every genocide that has been perpetrated, although it was clear what was happening in the first six stages, not enough people had the courage and will to intervene and prevent it reaching the seventh stage of mass killing. After the killing stops, the eighth stage of genocide is denial.

School students often discuss two related questions: whether the Holocaust could have been prevented and whether it could happen again. Because it has been perpetrated once, it can certainly be perpetrated again. For evil deeds to happen it only needs good people to look away. Most people are passive bystanders who look away and pretend they did not see. Until enough people become active upstanders and bear witness, protest and take action, there will be more genocide. Of course the Holocaust could have been prevented. The six stages of emerging and intensifying persecution against Jews, Roma and others that opposed Nazi orders, were clear for all to see. Too many good people closed their minds and refused to 'know' what they actually did know, whether out of prejudice or out of fear. They were not genocidaires but they colluded with the genocidaires by their inaction.

The easiest time to stop genocide is before the first stage of isolating and marginalizing a target group begins. That means blocking impunity by acknowledging and bringing to closure all previous genocide, and tackling prejudice with education and accurate information. But this is also the easiest time to be complacent and delude yourself that you need do nothing or that you can't do anything. One person can always do something and make a difference. The last major genocide, before the Holocaust, was perpetrated by the Ottoman Turks against the Christian Armenians and Greeks between 1915 and 1923. It is still continuing today in the eighth stage of denial. There is very little information about the Armenian Genocide because Modern Turkey denies it and threatens anyone who tries to exposes it. Too many people think it is out-dated and does not matter. Also, many who know about it decide to deny it out of self-interest, particularly politicians and business people who want to do business with Turkey. So, as there was no closure, Hitler was able to reassure his generals with impunity that nobody would care if they killed Jews and Roma.

Once the first stage has begun, it gets increasingly harder to stop the emerging genocide from progressing along the path that Greg Stanton has outlined. But it is still possible to intervene and prevent it reaching the stage of mass killing. Up until the outbreak of war in 1939, strong intervention might have prevented genocide against Roma and Jews, just as strong intervention before the 1914 war might have prevented genocide against the Christians of Anatolia. In both cases too few people cared and too many were prejudiced against the target group and denied knowing what was clearly evident. It takes courage to care enough to develop the will to act. Once war started there was probably no possibility of stopping the genocide in either case.

After the Second World War ended in 1945, the new post-war democratic government of Germany, almost immediately acknowledged the genocide against Jews and started making financial reparation, albeit reluctantly and under considerable pressure. But the German government denied that Roma were victims of Nazi genocide and continued to regard them as the 'social problem 'that the Nazis had labelled them. So no financial aid or reparation was forthcoming until a group of Roma forced the issue in 1980 by staging a hunger strike in the Dachau concentration camp, just outside Munich. In 1982 the Roma finally got their official acknowledgement that their ancestors had been victims of the brutal Nazi genocide. Some financial help followed and enabled them to create the Documentation and Cultural Centre of German Sinti and Roma in Heidelberg and stage a permanent exhibition of that genocide against Roma. This long period of German government denial, of the Nazi genocide against Roma and Sinti, allowed other European countries, such as Croatia, to deny their part in the genocide. It also allowed the whole of Europe, including Britain to continue regarding Roma as 'a social nuisance'. The appalling deprivation and persecution that Roma suffer all over Europe, and in other parts of the world, is largely a result of this denial. For the Roma, the eighth stage of genocide is continuing today and will do so until people care enough to protest and insist on genuine information instead of negatively biased media reportage and insulting TV programmes such as "My Big Fat Gypsy Wedding".

Unfortunately, it is much easier to remain in ignorance and nurse your prejudiced grievances. It takes courage and effort to challenge prejudice and search for the realities. And once you get to know about Roma, you discover that they are three dimensional people with feelings that are hurt and basic needs that are not being met and not the 'Gypsies' you have been duped into thinking they are. Once you know this, you can no longer be indifferent to their suffering; you can no longer blame them for what has been done to them. It is uncomfortable to give up indifference and begin to care enough to protest and support them as victims, not the law-breaking thieves you were taught to think they are. If we were to care and protest about all the deprived and ill-treated peoples in the world, our minds could not cope with it all, but we have responsibility towards our fellow members of the local community we live in.

On the whole it is easier to care about starving children in Africa, or other victimised groups far away, and send a cheque in the envelope provided with regularity by the Red Cross and other charities. We don't have to meet and see those people and it is not our doing that they suffer. But the Roma are part of our communities and it is our lack of action that allows them to be persecuted. As they are marginalized to live on the edges of society we can avoid seeing them most of the time and even pretend that they are not part of "Us" – but in reality they are part of our community and part of our population. I we tolerate them being treated unfairly, how can we claim our own rights?

What sort of society do we want to live in? Are we going to be seduced by 'the far right', EDL or BNP who want us to think, rather like the Nazis thought, that only certain people have a right to be in England or in Europe, and the rest should be driven out? Or do we want a community in which everyone is valued as a human being with equal rights?

Anxiety about lack of jobs, financial problems and government policies that we don't like makes us vulnerable to their slogans like "England for the English!" and we don't stop to think who they mean by 'the English'. That is exactly why

Holocaust education in school is so important. But learning needs to continue after school if we are going to get the most out of our lives while contributing the most we can to our community.

CHAPTER 10

CONCLUSION

"We live less than human lives if we think just of our own individual good" Dr. Rowan Williams, Archbishop of Canterbury, at the service for the Queens Jubilee, 2012

"Courage is what it takes to stand up and speak; courage is also what it takes to sit down and listen." Winston Churchill.

THIS BOOK IS not intended to impose my views on you, the reader, nor to prime you with loads of 'facts', but to offer ideas to think about. I hope reading it will have given you food for thought and, above all, inspired you to talk with and listen to more people and more authors so that you can come to an informed opinion that is really your own. I hope it has interested you enough to reach the insatiably questioning child inside you that is eager to explore the whole world but that may have got buried or stifled – or the child you once were if you are now an adult. I hope my book has roused your curiosity about a topic and a people that is so marginalized and excluded from our mainstream society that it is almost invisible and fulfils the proverb, "Out of sight – out of mind".

I have used a comparison with Jews, as Jews were marginalized and excluded from equal citizenship in their home countries all over the world for many centuries. Jews in Europe have experienced and come though what Roma and Travellers are still going through right now. They have yet to come through to being accepted as equal human beings and treated with respect and fairness. Because of this, perhaps Jews carry a little extra responsibility to protest at other peoples, like the Roma and Travellers who are still suffering blatant discrimination.

I find it hard to understand how anyone can fail to see a reflection of the Nazi Holocaust in the evictions and deportations, the burning of Roma campsites and the negative stereotypes of 'Gypsies', unless they close their eyes and hearts. But that is the nub of the problem. Hearts and minds are so often closed to many minority groups out of ignorance and prejudice. People who are ignorant and prejudiced tend to be vulnerable to fear. Fear of the unknown can be very powerful and a group of people you have never met can become terrifying due to the toxic misinformation of what other people, who may also have never met any of them, say about them. It becomes a vicious circle that can only be breached and dissolved by learning and reflection on what you hear and experience for yourself. That takes courage. It is tempting to take the easy way out and 'go along with the crowd'.

Human nature craves two unobtainable things – certainty and purity or perfection. We can have neither because the world we are all born into as Human Beings is designed for plurality and kaleidoscopic flux. That is why the world is so magnificent and beautiful – symbolised by the Garden of Eden. Insecurity and imperfection are in our human nature. Insecurity can make us fearful, prejudiced and antagonistic. It can also make us inventive and adventurous to seek and explore our planet and ourselves. Impurity can be experienced as threatening or shaming. It is also the source of rich variation that underlies adaptability and enables us to survive the ever-changing reality of the world we live in.

Prejudice and racism are not reasonable because they operate at a mental level that is not rational. Neuroscientists and psychologists tell us how the greater part of our mental functioning goes on below our awareness. Conscious mental action such as making reasoned decisions is only a small part of what goes on in our minds. Many of our decisions are made without our being aware of making them. Prejudice and racism fester in this area of mental activity we are not aware of until something bursts into our consciousness. That is why people often have no idea why they hate Roma or Jews or any other group as much as they do. No baby is born hating. Babies instinctively love whoever cares for them with love and kindness. But as they grow older, they learn to hate whatever the people around them hate; they learn it from parents, teachers, siblings and friends. We can sum it up as 'the myth of reasonable prejudice and the reality of the unreasonableness of racism'.

My explanations in this book are intended, not necessarily to convince you, but to make the ideas I present understandable. To make the ideas your own you will need to weigh them up in your mind, test them out in dialogue with other people and investigate to find more information that confirms or negates them. There is something dismissively insignificant about anti-Gypsy prejudice or Romaphobia. At the same time it is an ominous warning that those who ignore injustice to 'unimportant others' end up involved in gross injustice themselves. Pastor Martin Niemoeller's experience, and the poem he wrote to express it, is an example of this. The story and poem are in the Appendix.

The role of denial is very important in the sequence of ignorance leading to indifference and racism and finally to genocide. Denial of injustice while it is beginning, allows it to grow to monstrous proportions. It feeds on complacency and hearsay to nurture prejudice. That, in turn, spawns more and greater injustice that becomes blindly more and more 'acceptable' until it ripens into plans to get rid of the vilified and persecuted target group and becomes genocide.

I hope my book has stirred you to question yourself, your own motives and possible blindness, denial and prejudices - as well as questioning the ideas I have posed. Once you recognise injustice, to Roma or any other group, you remain an indifferent passive bystander until you do something to protest that it is unacceptable. When you protest you become an active upstander. The 1948 Universal Human Rights represent an important milestone in human development. Some people have not yet understood that these Human Rights are indivisible. You can't have 'more important' layers of society with more rights than less 'important' layers with fewer rights. A well functioning democracy respects its entire citizenry as equal by right.

Our democracy is likely to become corroded and destroyed unless we develop the courage to challenge the injustices that already exist and prevent more developing. The Roma and Travellers are not the problem; widespread ignorance about them generates misinformation, myths and prejudices. This leads people to insult and persecute Roma without knowing much about them. For example children who beg and steal are not necessarily 'criminals in the making' but are often victims of trafficking and appalling conditions they live in due to social marginalisation. In reality problems are caused by ignorance, prejudice and insensitivity of the majority population rather than by minority groups.

Speaking in 1993, Vaclav Havel prophetically remarked that "the treatment of the Roma is a litmus test for democracy". So far democracy has been found wanting. In my view, it is not democracy that is wanting but our own empathy and compassion to overcome indifference, apathy and unthinking prejudice.

But it is not all bad. The 'litmus test' shows some positive trends. There are increasing numbers of individual people and organisations that are dedicating their time and energy to improving the situation for Roma and Travellers and also challenging racism against minorities through education. A couple of examples are Maggie Smith Bendall who has been recognised in the Queen's birthday Honours with an OBE for her work helping Travellers and Roma in planning disputes; and Rene Cassin, the Jewish Philanthropic organisation, that is developing a project to raise awareness of Romaphobia. Also, some Roma who have educational achievements are using them to help their community. Siobhan Spencer, who identifies as a Gypsy and has an MBE for her community relations work, is using her University of Derby Law Degree to help Roma and Travellers.

Roma and Travellers are not as 'stand-off-ish' as many people like to think. Most of them respond well to being approached in friendship and treated decently. For example, in Blackpool, Roma responded to an invitation to join in an initiative to help to clean up flood damage. There is no reason to imagine that Roma and Travellers would not contribute richly to all areas of our society if we, the majority population, gave them opportunity and encouragement.

Finally, I hope that, on reaching the end of this book, the term 'Gypsy' has become somewhat strange to you and the umbrella names Roma and Travellers have become familiar.

PASTOR MARTIN NIEMOELLER

Pastor Niemoeller was head of a Christian church in Germany during Hitler's Third Reich, but he was not greedy for more power like Hitler was. He had the courage to challenge the Nazi claim that the State was above everything and to be obeyed by all. Niemoeller countered that God was above the state. For challenging Hitler, he was thrown into a concentration camp. When liberated after the end of the war, he wrote a moving poem:

> First they came for the trade unionists; I wasn't one and took no notice.
>
> Then they came for the communists; not being a communist I ignored it.
>
> Then they came for the Jews; as I wasn't Jewish I looked away and saw it not.
>
> Then they came for me and there was no-one left to stand up for me.

APPENDIX – NATIONAL ANTHEMS

THE ROMA NATIONAL ANTHEM

The Roma National Anthem was composed after WWII by Serbian-born Zurko Janovic, a talented balaika player, and officially adopted in 2004.

GELEM GELEM (Jelem Jelem)

I went, I went on long roads
I met happy Roma
O Roma where do you come from,
With tents on happy roads?

O Roma, O brothers

I once had a great family,
The Black Legions murdered them
Come with me Roma from all the world
For the Roma roads have opened
Now is the time, rise up Roma now,
We will rise high if we act

O Roma, O brothers

Open, God, Black doors
You can see where are my people.
Come back to tour the
Roads and walk with lucky Romani

O Roma, O brothers

Up, Gypsy! Now is the time
Come with me Roma
World, brown face and dark eyes
Much as I like black grapes

O Roma, O brothers

THE JEWISH NATIONAL ANTHEM

Ha Tikvah (The Hope) Tune by Samuel Cohen, an immigrant from Moldavia. Words written in 1886 by Naphtali Herz Imber, an English poet from Bohemia.

As long as the Jewish spirit is yearning deep in the heart,

With eyes turned toward the East, looking toward Zion,

Then our hope – the two thousand year old hope – will not be lost:

To be a free people in our land,

The land of Zion and Jerusalem

* * *

THE BRITISH NATIONAL ANTHEM

God Save the Queen (originally King), Composed by Thomas Augustine (1710-1788)

God save our gracious Queen,

Long live our noble Queen,

God save the Queen!

Send her victorious, Happy and Glorious,

Long to reign over us,

God save the Queen!

CHRONOLOGY OF THE NAZI PERSECUTION OF SINTI AND ROMA 'ZIGEUNER'

(This is taken from "Gypsy History in Germany and Neighbouring Lands: A Chronology to the Holocaust and Beyond" in "nationalities Papers", special issue on Gypsies)

1933: Nazi Law to legalise eugenic sterilisation 'to control Gypsies and Germans of black colour'.

1934: Nazi Laws forbidding Germans from marrying 'Jews, Gypsies and Negroes'.

1935: Strict Nazi criteria defining who is a Gypsy or a Jew.

1938: 'Gypsy clean-up week' in June – hundreds throughout Germany and Austria arrested, beaten and imprisoned.

1939: Nazi Racial Hygiene Office declared all Gypsies as 'hereditarily sick'.

1940: Nazis use 250 Romani children as 'guinea pigs' to test cyanide gas crystals in Buchenwald concentration camp.

1941: In July Reinhart Heydrich orders Einsatzkommandos to kill 'all Jews, Gypsies and mental patients'. 800 Roma are murdered in one 'Aktion' in the night of December 24th.

1944: In the night of August 1st/2nd 4,000 Sinti and Roma are gassed and incinerated at Auschwitz-Birkenau in one mass Aktion called the 'Zigeunernacht' (Gypsy night).

1945: By the end of the war between 70% and 8% of the Romani population of Europe had been annihilated by the Nazis. (This is a much higher than the proportion of the European Jewish population as comparably fewer Roma were able to escape abroad.) No Sinti or Roma were called to testify at the Nuremberg Trials along with Jews. Sinti and Roma were not recognised by the German government as victims of Nazism until 1982.

LURCHERS

Some people, mistakenly or out of prejudice, think Roma have big fierce dogs that will attack you for no reason. In fact most Lurchers are affectionate and friendly. They can act as guard dogs but that is not their main job. They were bred originally in Ireland for hunting rabbits and hares, as this is vital to a camping life. They are cross-bred, and therefore stronger and fitter than most pedigree dogs, from Sighthounds and sometimes Collies. Sighthounds are breeds of dogs that hunt with speed and sharp eye-sight as compared with hunting by scent. As they usually have some Greyhound in them,

Lurchers are long-legged, elegant, and energetic. But they also like to curl up beside you on the couch while you watch TV.

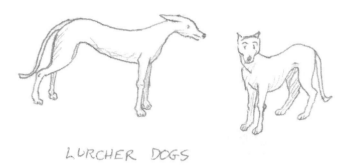

LURCHER DOGS

SOME IDEAS FOR INTERESTING LEARNING

Look up the story of Ceferino Giminez Malle, the Roma Saint called El Pele, on the Internet.

Look up "Genocide Watch" on the Internet and make sure you understand the difference between war and genocide.

The Holocaust Explained: www.theholocaustexplained.org

Subscribe to Travellers Times @£14 per year – four copies annually:www.travellerstimes.org.uk

Subscribe (free) to the Roma Virtual Network:

www.valery-novoselsky.org/romavirtualnetwork.html   or
romale@zahav.net.il

Contact your own local MP and your local council and find out what they are planning for the next Holocaust Memorial day, and are they including acknowledgement of the Nazi genocide against the Sinti and Roma. Find out, also, what provision there is for Roma and Travellers in your Borough or County Council: do they get equality of housing, education and health services? If you have the chance to go to Germany and spend a little time in Heidelberg, visit the Documentation and Cultural Centre of the Central Council of German Sinti and Roma. There is a very moving exhibition of the Nazi genocide against Roma and Sinti. You can contact the Centre at number 2 Bremmeneckgasse, 69117 Heidelberg Germany, or ring them on 49-6221-981 102 (or email info@sintiundroma.de). They will send you information and books in English or German. A very informative little book by Romani Rose, "Roma and Sinti – Human Rights for Europe's Largest Minority" is highly recommended as it tells the story of how the Documentation and Cultural Centre was founded.

BOOKS BY AND ABOUT ROMA AND GYPSIES

Books by Romanies:

Ceija Stojka: *Traueme ich, dass ich lebe?* Random House, 2009

Walter Winter: *Winter Time: Memoirs of a Sinto who Survived Auschwitz*, University of Herts, 2004

Toby Sonneman: *Shared Sorrows: a Gypsy Family remembers the Holocaust*, University of Herts, 2002.

Yvonne Slee: *Torn Away Forever*, Amber Press, 2005

Maggie Smith-Bendall: *Rabbit Stew and a Penny or Two*, Abacus, 2009

Isobel Fonseca: *Bury Me Standing*, Vitage, 1996

"The Living Fire" by Ronald Lee, Magoria Books, 2009

Books about Roma and Travellers:

Ian Hancock: *We are the Romani People*, University of Herts, 2002

Jan Yoors: *Crossing: A Journal of Survival and Resistance in WWII*, Waveland Press, 1988

Colum McCann: *Zoli* (based on the legendary Polish Romani Papusza)

Donald Kenrick & Grattan Puxon: *Gypsies Under the Swastika*, University of Herts, 2009

From Race Science to Camps: the Gypsies during the Second World War, Gypsy Research Centre, University of Herts, 1997

Films about Roma and Travellers:

My Big Fat Gypsy Stereotype, 15 min DVD obtainable from the East Sussex Traveller Education Service.

Porrajmos, 15 min. DVD obtainable from Plymouth & Devon Racial Equality Council

Forgotten Genocide, a digital exhibition on the Internet at www.romasinti.eu

Requiem for Auschwitz: A full orchestral requiem dedicated to all victims of Auschwitz, by the Sinti & Roma Philharmonic Orchestra of Frankfurt, written by Roger Moreno Rathgeb, conducted by Riccardo Sahiti. Online at: rromaniconnect.org.

Organisations that offer learning material about the Holocaust:

Materials and events offered by all these can be found via their websites:

The Holocaust Centre at Beth Shalom, The Holocaust Memorial Day Trust, The Holocaust Education Trust, The London Jewish Cultural Centre, The Jewish Museum, The Imperial War Museum, The Wiener Library.

Organisations that offer learning material about Roma and Porrajmos:

The National Association of Teachers of Traveller children (NATT+)

Online at: rromaniconnect.org. and Romasintiholocaust.html

ABOUT THE AUTHOR

Ruth Barnett is a happily married mother of three children with two grandchildren, and a former teacher and psychotherapist. Having escaped the Nazi plans to exterminate Jews and Gypsies by coming to England on the Kindertransport at age four, she now devotes her time and energy to speaking in schools, colleges, conferences and any group that invites her. She says "I have no right to protest against anti-Semitism unless I also protest at other peoples being targeted through prejudice and hatred". In her childhood in rural England, Ruth Barnett knew Gypsies as respected and welcomed itinerant agricultural and craft workers. Today, although as illegal as anti-Semitism and Islamophobia, the last bastion of culturally acceptable racism is against Roma and Traveller Gypsies.

30912459R00084